BEYOND RACE AND GENDER

BEYOND RACE AND GENDER

Unleashing the Power of Your Total Work Force by Managing Diversity

R. ROOSEVELT THOMAS, Jr.

American Management Association

Library of Congress Cataloging-in-Publication Data

Thomas, R. Roosevelt.
    Beyond race and gender : unleashing the power of your total work
force by managing diversity / R. Roosevelt Thomas, Jr.
    p.   cm.
    Includes bibliographical references (p.   ) and index.
    ISBN 0-8144-5014-8
    1. Minorities—Employment   2. Women—Employment.
3. Personnel management.   4. Corporate culture.
5. Organizational change.
I. Title.   II. Title: Managing diversity.
HF5549.5.M5T46   1991   90-56412
658.3—dc20   CIP

Printing number

10   9   8   7   6   5   4   3   2   1

This book is dedicated to
    my wife, **Ruby**
    our children, **Shane, April,** and **Jarred**
    my mother, **Icye Potts Thomas**
    my grandmother, the late **Lela Margaret Potts**
    my father, **Rufus R. Thomas, Sr.**
    my aunt, **Sara Potts**
    my brother, **Robert,** and his wife, **Carol,** and
        their children, **T.J.** and **Jason**

Contents

Foreword

Managing diversity is an idea whose time has come. More and more, corporations and organizations of all kinds are awakening to the fact that a diverse work force is not a burden, but their greatest potential strength—when managed properly.

One reason for the awakening is the increasingly diverse marketplace of this country. Who can best understand and serve this changed and changing market? Certainly not the "old-boy network." It takes a diverse work force at all levels of the company, including senior management.

A second and even more urgent reason for the interest in managing diversity is the stark facts of demographics. The growth in the U.S. labor force now and for the foreseeable future will be largely composed of women, minorities, and immigrants. They will constitute about 85 percent of the new entrants in the work force, according to the landmark Hudson Institute Study.

Companies now realize they must attract, retain, and promote this full spectrum of people just to keep the business running. So great is their need that advice on the management of diversity has suddenly become a growth industry.

But the author of this book understood the need years ago, long before the subject started appearing in business periodicals and seminar agendas. When Dr. Roosevelt Thomas formed the American Institute for Managing Diversity in 1983, his was a voice in the wilderness. But gradually, he began to be heard. A few companies, including Avon, turned to him—in our case out of urgent need. More and more companies followed suit, and today the voice of Roosevelt is heard—and listened to—in boardrooms throughout the land.

Now, *the* pioneer in the field of managing diversity has written *the* definitive work on the subject. It deserves to be read—and read carefully—by everyone responsible for the future of every organization.

I believe in Roosevelt's theories of managing diversity because I've seen them work.

In the mid-1980s, Avon was typical of companies that were trying to bring minorities and women into what we were pleased to call the "mainstream." We had special recruiting programs. We had mentoring, tracking, interning, in-house training—all supported by a strong commitment from top management.

But our programs weren't working as we'd expected. We did succeed in attracting minorities and women into the company. But they seldom moved up, and their turnover was high. We were making some progress, but it was painfully slow.

In retrospect, it's clear that we were making a fundamental error. We weren't really *valuing* diversity, much less *managing* it. We were merely trying "to do the right thing." We were inviting minorities and women to join and blend into our corporate culture. But most people, no matter what their background, don't want to blend into anything. They want to be themselves—preserve their own culture, heritage, and customs. They don't think "being themselves" should deny them equal opportunity. And they're right.

At Avon, we realized we needed a whole new approach. And in the mid-1980s, in the depths of our frustration, we had the great good fortune to discover Roosevelt. In counseling our top management group, he explained that it was the culture of the *company* that had to change, not the culture of the *people*. He brought new resonance to an idea I'd been toying with for some time—that America is not a melting pot, but a great mosaic where all the nationalities of the world have come to lend their hues and tints to the beauty that is America . . . be it in art, music, philosophy, skills, food, or commerce. And the successful organization must reflect that same mosaic.

That's another theme that has been on the ascendancy recently. To a great many business, social, and political leaders, it makes sense.

As we at Avon began to send our mid-level managers to the Institute's training sessions at Morehouse College, we made measurable progress in attracting, retaining, and promoting the minorities and women whose abilities we so desperately needed. Roosevelt tells the Avon story in Chapter 7. As for me, I became so enthusiastic about his programs that I accepted the invitation to become the Institute's first board chairman—a richly rewarding experience that I'll always cherish.

As you read this book, don't look for glib solutions. There are no eight or ten easy steps to understanding and managing diversity. You can't change a culture overnight when it's been in place for decades. Avon, for instance, has not reached the pinnacle of corporate multiculturalism. We'd like to be there. We're working on it. We're making progress.

While the book offers no easy answers, it does offer insights and practical methodology that will, over time, build a better and more diverse culture in your organization. And not incidentally, it will help you build a competitive advantage that will last for years to come.

James E. Preston
Chief Executive Officer
Avon Products, Inc.

Preface

Several years ago when I served as dean of the Atlanta University Graduate School of Business Administration, a corporate manager asked why we did not develop "something" to help white males manage their black employees. This suggestion led me down a long road of inquiry and ultimately resulted in *Beyond Race and Gender*.

My first reaction to the notion of helping white males manage blacks was mixed. I wondered why there was a need for special assistance with blacks. Weren't they people like everyone else? Why wouldn't what worked with others work with blacks? In a real sense, I was offended by the suggestion that extra help was required for blacks.

But after considerable thought and research, I realized that all corporations—regardless of the quality of their affirmative action efforts—were concerned about upward mobility and retention of blacks. As a means of testing the proposal to develop a special program, I undertook a review of the literature to see what had been reported about the experiences of blacks in corporate America. I made two discoveries.

One, only a few writers looked at the experiences of blacks—or women—from a *managerial* perspective; instead they peered from the perspectives of race relations, interpersonal relations, or legal, moral, or social responsibility. Very few researchers started with the view of determining the implications for a manager seeking to create a corporate environment that would work for *everyone*.

Two, most of the available works described the experience of blacks and women in corporate America and offered them advice for being successful. These efforts were mainly aimed at helping blacks and women understand their circumstances and challenges and preparing them for effective assimilation into the mainstream.

All of this said to me that here was an unfilled need: to understand through systematic research the managerial experience of managers with blacks and women so that insights could be gained as to how white males might better manage them. I defined management as the use of various managerial tools to enable people to practice the behavior required for achieving corporate objectives. Here more was meant than race relations or interpersonal relations. Beyond these matters were the issues of creating an appropriate corporate culture and set of organizational systems.

Stated differently, I was suggesting implicitly that a white male manager could be free of discrimination and could have excellent interpersonal relations with women and blacks, and still not know how to manage them—still not know how to create a culture with appropriate related systems that would work for them *and* white males. Once I became aware of this implicit reasoning, I became even more convinced that the managerial perspective and its implications had not been explored.

With this framework in mind, I approached Hugh Gloster, the president of Morehouse College, in 1983 about starting up an applied research center for the purpose of exploring this managerial perspective. He agreed, and we formed the American Institute for Managing Diversity (initially known as the Institute for Corporate Leadership and Management at Morehouse College).

Shortly after launching the Institute, I came across studies previewing what eventually would become *Workforce 2000*, the widely discussed report prepared by the Hudson Institute and the Department of Labor. These preliminary glimpses led to three conclusions:

1. The issues I proposed to research applied to minorities in general, and not just blacks. So I broadened our focus to include other minorities and women.
2. Not only would white male managers have to manage people not like themselves, but all managers would face this challenge. So I aimed our assistance at *all* managers, not just white male managers.

3. Employees differ not just on the basis of race, gender, and ethnicity, but also on a variety of other dimensions such as age, functional and educational backgrounds, tenure with the organization, lifestyles, and geographic origins—just to name a few. I believed that these dimensions and others had to be included when considering work force "diversity."

These conclusions set me on a course to tease out a definition of managing diversity that was different from the traditional affirmative action approach. Specifically, I sought to address the following question: "As a manager goes about enabling/influencing/empowering his/her work force, and as that work force becomes increasingly diverse, are there things that have to be done differently (managerially speaking) with a diverse work force than would be the case with a homogeneous work force?"

Fundamentally, it is a question we in this country have not addressed—but one that we must, for it has profound strategic implications for individual corporations and our nation as a whole. If we are unable to create organizations that will work *naturally* for everyone, we will have great difficulty tapping the potential of our human resources.

The notion of *Beyond Race and Gender* does not call for ignoring race and gender factors, but for recognizing that they are part of a larger, even more complex, picture and that sustainable progress with these issues in corporations will have to be based on the managerial perspective. Further, the notion does not call for abandoning the traditional affirmative action perspective grounded in motives of legal, moral, and social responsibility, *but rather for the expansion* of this perspective.

Beyond Race and Gender presents the results of six years of developing a working definition of managing diversity. It is intended for managers seeking to achieve sustainable progress with diversity issues and to gain a competitive advantage for their organizations. Companies that move on this front now will be ideally positioned to make giant competitive strides. This book is intended to facilitate the process.

—R. Roosevelt Thomas, Jr.

Acknowledgments

A number of individuals facilitated the writing of this book.

My wife and our children provided support and understanding throughout the effort. I very much appreciate this encouragement.

Morehouse College's leadership, including President-Emeritus Hugh M. Gloster and President Leroy Keith, has been supportive of the creation and development of The American Institute for Managing Diversity. Dr. Gloster authorized the founding of the Institute as an affiliate of the College, while Dr. Keith has fostered efforts during his tenure to realize The Institute's potential as a national asset.

My mother and grandmother have always in very quiet, but firm and positive ways nurtured my growth along a number of lines.

Over the past seven years, hundreds of executives, managers, and professionals have listened to my ideas on diversity and have responded in a manner that has furthered my thinking. In a very real sense, this book could not have been written without them.

Executives at Avon Products, Inc. and the company referred to here as Culberson Industries granted permission to report their experiences with diversity.

The members of The American Institute for Managing Diversity's Board of Trustees and Advisory Council have been a source of encouragement from the launching of The Institute to the present. I owe a special thanks to Larry Baytos (formerly of Quaker Oats) and Jim Preston (Avon Products, Inc.), respectively chairman and former chairman of the Board, and also to Jim Daniels (The Hartford Insurance Company), who has served as president of the Advisory Council since its beginning.

The Executive Leadership Council funded the research leading to the chapter on total quality and managing diversity, and granted permission for inclusion of the material.

The *Harvard Business Review* gave permission to include excerpts from my article "From Affirmative Action to Affirming Diversity" (copyright 1990, President and Fellows of Harvard College, March-April 1990).

Larry Baytos, Robert L. Davis, Yvonne Jackson, Eugene Jones, Terri Kruzan, Robert L. Lattimer, and Kathy Lee read and commented on earlier drafts. Kathy Lee provided a helpful sounding board for our thinking on managing change.

Adrienne Hickey, senior acquisitions and planning editor, and her colleagues at AMACOM, have provided effective, professional facilitative assistance.

Shirley Manor typed the several drafts of the manuscript in a pleasant, competent and proficient manner. I am most appreciative.

Since the birth of The Institute, Debra Francis has brought commitment and a sense of continuity to our work.

Marjorie Woodruff assisted with organizing the initial drafts.

I thank the support staffs of the American Institute for Managing Diversity and Diversity Consultants, Inc. for their general assistance.

To all of these individuals and organizations, I offer my profound thanks.

Chapter 1

Up Against the Limits

A young corporation with a vibrant business concept is growing rapidly—too rapidly. Several factions are emerging: founding employees vs. "post-founding" hires, new-building occupants vs. old-building occupants, function x vs. function y, home office vs. field offices, male vs. female, and minority vs. white.

The founders see this splintering, but they are not sure what to do. They are not prepared to deal with management issues; they are far more comfortable with entrepreneurial activity. The company, which all recognize has enormous potential, is on the verge of detonating.

||||||||||||||||||||

Company A is an established maker of minicomputers and mainframes; it has been around for a long time and is known as a solid, respectable member of the high-tech "old guard." It's a white-shirt—and—tie kind of place. Company B is a software company, just a few years past startup stage, with a strong reputation for creative and somewhat flashy innovations. Most employees are young, ambitious, and dedicated; they are prone to blue jeans and running shoes.

Company A, hoping to increase overall revenue by diversifying into this obviously related area, buys the much smaller Company B. They're expecting a synergistic new entity that will make more money than the two original companies did. But instead, the results for the first two years are considerably *less* than the two companies were making separately. The problem? The cultures of the two companies were so very different that the people couldn't work well to-

1

gether. They spent too much time in power struggles and political maneuverings and not enough time developing product.

||||||||||||||||||||

A light manufacturing facility in the Midwest has a policy of promoting floor supervisors from within. When the company started, its work force came from the local community, which was mostly white families who were second- or third-generation Scandinavians; thus the current supervisors, promoted from that original work force, are mostly white men in their fifties. The current work force is still drawn from the local area but the demographics have changed, and there is now a large Southeast Asian population in the community. Supervisors have tried to get new employees to do things the "right" way, and no one can figure out why productivity is so low.

||||||||||||||||||||

A new suburban church, founded as a nondenominational organization, attracted members from a variety of denominations. For a time, there was harmony. But before long, individual members began to push for traditions and practices that they had experienced in their own denominations. The various practices were at odds with each other, and with the nondenominational concept. Some members felt that the church had tilted too much toward one particular denomination. In the resulting tension, many members left the church.

||||||||||||||||||||

A regional public utility in the Southwest has a strong reputation with the general public as being particularly sensitive to recruiting and hiring minorities; its managers have won numerous awards for affirmative action programs. But their turnover rate of minority employees is three times that of whites, and race-related morale problems are becoming severe. In an atmosphere of distrust and anxiety, quality of work is suffering.

These situations are quite varied, and yet there is one common thread: the people who make up the population of the organizations—the members of the church, the employees of the several businesses—are different from one another. They are also similar in some respects, and there are no doubt many lessons to be learned from their experiences, but it is their differences with which we are here concerned.

Some of the differences are easy to identify, for they are visible right on the surface: individuals are male or female, young or old, white or minority. Other differences are not so easy to see: education level, lifestyle, goals and ambitions, sexual orientation, personal values and belief systems involving loyalty to authority, commitment to the organization's vision, ways of thinking, and respect (or fear) for new ideas.

Within any one organization, you might find representatives of several of these groups: some who are inclined to push against authority, some who are very cautious with change, some with an entrepreneurial, "loner" style, some who flourish in a team setting. And you would probably see women and men of several different races and ethnic groups: white, black, Asian, Hispanic, native American. This mix is termed "diversity." The more different groups there are represented in any one organization, the more diverse that organization is.

Those at the helm of these organizations have a choice: they can treat all members as if they were the same (or try to force them to *become* the same), or they can view the diversity as an opportunity, a strategic lever. If they take the first course, they risk seriously jeopardizing the strength of the organization, possibly its very survival. If they take the second course—and if they do so before the competition does—they will have an enormous strategic advantage.

The Tough Realities of the 1990s

Diversity as an issue is new. It became an issue when three powerfully significant trends reached their own critical points at about the same time:

1. The global market in which American corporations must now do business became intensely competitive.
2. The makeup of the U.S. work force began changing dramatically, becoming more diverse.

3. Individuals began to increasingly celebrate their differences and become less amenable to compromising what makes them unique. This inclination represents a marked departure from previous times when predispositions were to "fit in."

To succeed in this highly competitive environment, managers must find ways to get the highest level of contribution from their workers. And they will not be able to do that unless they are aware of the many ways that their understanding of diversity relates to how well, or how poorly, people contribute.

Worldwide Competition

It is not necessary here to document the battering that U.S. companies have taken from overseas and domestic competitors, or to describe the climate of competitiveness that drives so many major corporate decisions. This competition is not going to go away; it is only going to increase, as American companies continue their scramble for markets.

The point for us to remember is that, at the same time, they are scrambling for the best talent they can find. And searching for ways to get the best from the employees they now have. That is at the core of the business rationale for thinking about diversity. Managers must be clear about this; everything this book has to say about diversity is grounded in this business rationale: to thrive in an increasingly unfriendly marketplace, companies must make it a priority to create the kind of environment that will attract the best new talent and will make it possible for employees to make their fullest contribution.

Changing Demographics

The leaders of U.S. corporations must also recognize that the makeup of the overall American work force today is vastly different from what it was when they started in business. And this change, too, is only going to continue.

Workforce 2000 has projected that from 1985 to 2000 minorities, women, and immigrants will compose 85 percent of the growth in the work force.[1] *Workforce 2000* projects the highest rate of increase for Asian Americans and Hispanics; however, Asian Americans will be less significant numerically than Hispanics because they are growing from a much smaller base. The labor participation growth rate of white women will be relatively smaller, but because they are expanding from a large base, the increase will be numerically substantial (see Exhibit 1-1).

By way of perspective, it's important to remember that the projection refers to work force *growth*. It doesn't mean that the prominence of white males in the labor force will change dramatically. In 1985, for example, white males composed 49 percent of the labor force; by 2000, they will constitute approximately 45 percent.

Still, in a number of companies, women and minorities already compose large portions of the existing work force and as

Exhibit 1-1. Rate of growth of labor force composition (1986–2000).

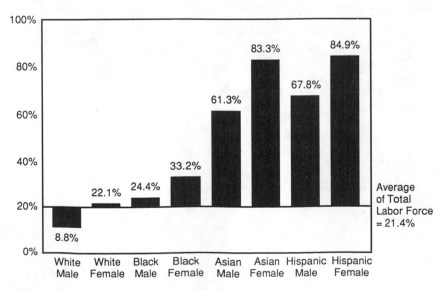

Source: Bureau of Labor Statistics, March 1988.

much as 80 percent of new-hires. For managers of these corporations, the future is now.

Labor Shortage

An equally significant prediction is that overall the work force will grow at a declining rate. As Exhibit 1-2 reflects, for the decade ending in 1990, the projected growth rate was 27 percent; for the decade ending in the year 2000, it is 11 percent.

One important implication of our changing demographics is the very real potential for a labor shortage. Managers are expected to experience increasing difficulty in meeting their staffing needs. Primarily, this is because the individuals composing the bulk of the work force *growth* historically have been underrepresented in the occupations where the greatest growth is projected: the health professions, natural sciences, computer science, mathematics, and engineering.

According to current trends, managers of all organizations can anticipate a time when the potential labor force will consist of

Exhibit 1-2. Percentage increase in the labor force (1940–2000).

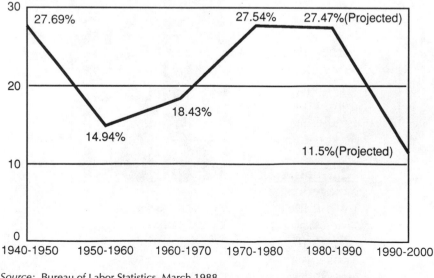

Source: Bureau of Labor Statistics, March 1988.

large numbers of minorities and women who will be willing and physically able to work but will lack the necessary skills to take advantage of occupational opportunities. This scenario has been called the "skills gap." Exacerbating this situation will be the anticipated surge in baby-boomer retirements. The combined circumstances hold the potential for a very real labor crunch.

The End of Assimilation

Some may wonder what all the fuss is about. Haven't there always been workers of different races, different ethnic backgrounds? Isn't the melting pot the American way?

Traditionally, the American approach to diversity has been assimilation. Newcomers are expected to adapt so that they "fit"; the burden of making the change falls to them. This is true for the business world as well as society as large. Managers have insisted that people who are different bear the brunt of adjusting, and they have been more than willing to help employees through the process. In effect, managers tell new employees:

> We have determined in this company that there is a specific culture, and that people who fit a given mold do better than those who do not. As you join us, we're going to hold up a mirror in front of you. In this mirror, you will note that we have sketched the outline of the mold that works here. If you fit, fine, come on in. If you don't, we invite you to allow us to shape you to the appropriate mold. This is for our mutual benefit, as it will help to ensure that you have a productive relationship with the company.

The assimilation model has been so acceptable in the past that many managers tend to take it for granted. They believe that their company's culture evolved over the years in response to business realities, and it seems only reasonable that employees be expected to conform. Assimilation is what ensures unity and common purpose; without it, there would be chaos.

Employees, too, have "bought into" the rationale for assimilation. In anticipation of promised success as a result of conforming, they have dropped their ethnic and gender identity at the door of the corporation.

"I Don't Want to Assimilate"

But times—and employee attitudes—are changing. Simply put, people are less willing to be assimilated, even for eight hours of the day. Increasingly, prospective employees are saying, "I'm different, and proud of what makes me so. I can help your team, and I would like to join you, but only if I can do so without compromising my uniqueness." And, as we have just seen, it's a seller's market for skills.

This reluctance to change is becoming apparent in several employee groups. It's true for new minority employees, who observe that their predecessors who "fitted in" have lost some of their "minority identity." It's true for new women employees, who see their predecessors wondering if the "loss of femininity" has been too great a cost to pay for success. It's true for young workers, who find themselves questioning the wisdom of old men with out-of-date experience and see little value in learning to be like them. It's true for highly educated professionals, who come to their companies with expectations of participatory decision making quite at odds with the usual hierarchical style. All of them, in their own way, are saying, "Don't assimilate me. Don't dilute my strengths."

The Danger of Assimilation

I am not suggesting the elimination of all assimilation; some willingness to adapt will always be required. But wise managers must realize that enforced assimilation is not only largely unattainable, it is also bad for business.

People being assimilated are never quite comfortable. They often find themselves caught between two worlds and uncomfortable in both. What is perhaps more damaging, forcing everyone to assimilate leaves untapped potential. Because assimilating people want to fit in, they focus on doing the expected or accommodating the norm, on playing it safe. They avoid offering suggestions that would make them stand out. They can't focus on their personal strengths or on innovative ideas; they're too busy trying to adapt. The consequences can be a lackluster performance. In a competitive environment, assimilation is stifling and deadly.

Burning the Available Fuel

In a nutshell, then, the leaders of America's corporations face a double dilemma: they are struggling against a level of competition that was unheard of twenty years ago, and their primary resource for fighting that competition—their pool of talented and committed workers—is changing dramatically in ways that are baffling to many. What exactly does all this mean for corporate America?

A good way to picture the implications of these changes is to imagine yourself driving around your hometown burning your usual brand of gasoline. Imagine that I tell you that by the end of the next twelve months, the only fuel available to you will be a mixture that is 15 percent gasoline and 85 percent something else.

You have a choice. You can ignore my projection and continue to drive as usual. But if you do, and I'm right, your car will eventually grind to a halt, with perhaps terminal damage to the engine. Or you can monitor closely the mixture offered by your favorite service station and adjust—or even change—your motor to ensure that you can burn whatever fuel you can get.

Burning the increasingly diverse human resource fuel is the challenge that faces all of institutional America. We have only begun to address this task. If we don't learn to burn all the fuel—to unleash the power that all the various groups in our national work force have to offer—we will compromise all our institutions, business, academic, religious, governmental, and civic.

A New Approach to Diversity

The increasing diversity of the American work force is a fact. Those who try to force today's reality into yesterday's management patterns will seriously jeopardize the viability of their enterprise. Those who see it as an opportunity for competitive advantage can outrun their competition if they are willing to take on the challenge.

What is required is a new way of thinking about diversity, not as an "us/them" kind of problem to be solved but as a resource to be managed. That is what we are about here: *managing diversity*.

Let's start with a definition:

> Managing diversity is a comprehensive managerial process for developing an environment that works for all employees.

Defining managing diversity as a *process* highlights its evolutionary nature. It allows corporations to develop (evolve) steps for generating a *natural* capability to tap the potential of all employees. *All* employees, including the white male.

Another word for the process of tapping employees' full potential is "empowerment"—a term you have been hearing a lot about recently. In fact, a managing diversity capability is implicit in several innovations already in process in progressive organizations. Some corporations, for example, are moving to "push decision making down." Others are implementing "total quality" initiatives. Still others have downsized their work forces in search of greater efficiency and productivity. All of these initiatives, however they differ, have one aspect in common: Their success depends on the ability to empower the total work force. In the context of a diverse work force, this circumstance means that managing diversity becomes a critical determinant of success.

The Full Scope of Diversity

Diversity includes everyone; it is not something that is defined by race or gender. It extends to age, personal and corporate background, education, function, and personality. It includes lifestyle, sexual preference, geographic origin, tenure with the organization, exempt or nonexempt status, and management or nonmanagement. It also shows up clearly with companies involved in acquisitions and mergers. In this expanded context, white males are as diverse as their colleagues. A commitment to diversity is a commitment to all employees, not an attempt at preferential treatment.

Here are some typical situations that illustrate these broader dimensions of diversity.

- One manufacturing manager has told me: "People talk a lot about race and gender, but for us, the biggest diversity issue is between senior and junior white male managers. They simply don't understand each other. They have different lifestyles, agendas, and priorities. Put them on the same team, and they can't seem to get along."

- A company with facilities in the South moved a key manager from its North Carolina operation to its Alabama plant. Even though the Alabama facility was in the midst of economic crisis and presumably needed all the help it could get, it took the transferred manager two years to be fully accepted. He was, after all, a Tar Heel in Crimson Tide country.

- Differences in lifestyle and perspective separate "liberated" women from those with more traditional perspectives. When they serve as support personnel, they differ greatly in their relationship with their bosses. Traditionally oriented women tend to draw an analogy to the family; they view their bosses as the head of the household, and they take on the role of wife. Liberated women, however, see the boss as simply a supervisor, and they expect to be treated as professionals.

- During the process leading to the merger of Time, Inc., and Warner Communications, the *Los Angeles Times* reported on a clash over corporate culture at a court hearing.[2] We don't always recognize that mergers and acquisitions produce diversity problems. Yet this article reflects two important truths: that mergers and acquisitions represent a union of two cultures and that the management of this union can make or break the merger.

Managing Diversity vs. the Traditional Approach

As a way of thinking about human resources, managing diversity is new. And it is very different from traditional business perspectives.

- Managing diversity means approaching diversity at three levels simultaneously: individual, interpersonal, and organizational. The traditional focus has been on individual and interpersonal aspects alone. What is new is seeing diversity as an issue for the entire organization, involving the very way organizations are structured.
- Managing diversity approaches diversity from a *management* perspective. That is, it deals with the way organizations are managed, the way managers do their jobs. It is grounded in a very specific definition of "managing": creating an environment that allows the people being managed to reach their full potential. At its best, it means getting from employees not only everything you have a right to expect, but everything they have to offer.
- Managing diversity requires that line managers learn a new way. They are asked to spend less time "doing" the work and more time enabling employees to do the work. (There is more about this doer/enabler spectrum in Chapter 3.)
- Managing diversity defines diversity broadly; it addresses the many ways employees are different *and* the many ways they are alike. Managing diversity goes beyond race and gender, and includes many other dimensions (more about this in Chapter 2). It is not about white males managing women and minorities; it is about all managers empowering whoever is in their work force.
- Managing diversity assumes that adaptation is a two-way street, a mutual process between the individual and the company. This is a change from the usual assimilation approach, where the burden of adapting rests solely on the individual who is different.
- Unlike more familiar approaches, managing diversity is not a program, not an orchestrated set of actions designed to "do" something. It calls for more than changing individual behaviors. It requires a fundamental change in the corporation's way of life. Implementing it takes many years.

Corporate Culture: The Root of the Matter

How any given organization chooses to view its employees is very much a matter of the organization's culture. That seems quite obvious on the surface, but it has significant implications for managing diversity. In fact, we cannot understand the concept of managing diversity—much less begin to implement it—without a full appreciation of its linkage to culture.

Edgar H. Schein, noted organizational psychologist, has defined corporate culture as the basic assumptions driving life in a given organization.[3]

It is important to understand that these assumptions are *unexamined*. That makes them different from values, which often are articulated and debated. They are also different from behaviors, styles of working, and traditions. Those things are outward manifestations of deep, fundamental understandings about how the organization works.

One way to understand culture is to conceptualize an organization as a tree (see Exhibit 1-3). In this organizational tree, the roots are the corporation's culture. These roots, of course, are below the surface, invisible. But they give rise to the trunk, branches, and leaves—the visible parts of the tree. Nothing can take place in the branches and be sustained naturally unless it is congruent with the roots.

By way of analogy, assume that I live in Georgia and own a

Exhibit 1-3. Culture as tree roots.

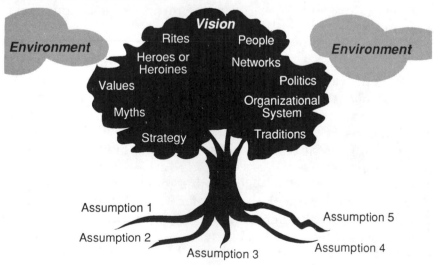

grove of oak trees. I like these trees; they provide an enormous amount of pleasure to me. But I would also like to see peaches come into season. So I buy some peach trees and bring them to the grove. Unfortunately, there isn't enough space to plant the new trees without removing some of the oaks, and I don't want to do this.

I decide instead to graft a healthy peach limb onto one of the oak trees. I begin the process, controlling for moisture, light, temperature, and anything else that might affect the grafting effort. And, for a while, it seems as if I've been successful.

Then peach season arrives, and the limb produces one very puny peach. I, however, am encouraged; we are headed in the right direction. My encouragement is ill-founded, however. The tree knows better. The roots of the oak are sending signals to the peach limb. "This," they are saying, "is an oak tree. Despite all of Roosevelt's efforts, you will wither, die, and fall off. Peach limbs don't grow on oaks."

We will visit this tree again; it has much to teach us.

Getting Started

Managing diversity is a complex, multifaceted, and time-consuming process. But it is possible to describe the heart of the process in a very few words. In overview, the process of managing diversity entails:

- Examining an organization's corporate culture
- Identifying those elements of the culture that are fundamental, the "roots" from which corporate behaviors spring
- Determining whether the roots support or hinder the aspirations for managing diversity
- Changing the cultural roots that are hindrances

The chapters that follow will examine these ingredients in some detail. We will look at the various facets of managing diversity, explore the ways it differs from traditional approaches, examine its significance and potential benefits, indicate the principal factors that hinder implementation, and provide practical suggestions for its successful implementation. Pioneering efforts of two companies are detailed in later chapters.

This is not, however, a "how to" manual. Remember, managing diversity is not a program, it is a process; it doesn't lend itself to step-by-step how-tos. Furthermore, it is still very much in an embryonic state, and there is little pragmatic case material. Instead, the book explores the concept—its nuances, its complexities, and its potential benefits.

The book requires that action-oriented managers possess a willingness to do something different: to postpone action in the interest of gaining understanding. This understanding will, I believe, reap big rewards. It will empower you as a manager by giving you the perspective you need to handle a dramatically changing work force.

Managing diversity is not for everyone. It requires either vision or pain. If your company is experiencing pain with diversity issues at this time, you can appreciate the value of this approach. Similarly, corporations that have a vision of the future and an understanding of the implications of the changes in work force demographics and in employee attitudes can understand the opportunities presented by managing diversity.

Organizations that have such a vision have a big head start over those that do not. To state the matter in blunt business terms: who do you want to see attract the best talent and reap the benefits of greater productivity, you or your competitors? Make no mistake, diversity issues are corporate imperatives of the greatest magnitude.

Chapter Two

Beyond Traditional Approaches

It is perhaps easier to understand and fully appreciate the concept of managing diversity by comparing it to two other approaches that are similar but more familiar—affirmative action and valuing differences.

In our nation, we have traditionally thought of diversity in the context of legal or moral imperatives. Within organizations, diversity can be addressed from several different perspectives, each with a different agenda:

- *Civil Rights:* Seeks to end discrimination and racism and to comply with legal requirements. Asks this basic question, "What do civil rights-related laws guarantee our employees?"
- *Women's Rights:* Focuses on eliminating sexism. The principal question is, "What can be done to eliminate discrimination against women?"
- *Humanitarianism:* Based on a view of the human race as a brotherhood. Seeks to foster good relations through enhanced tolerance, acceptance, and understanding of individual differences. The driving question is, "What can be done to enhance relations among all peoples for the good of the human species?"
- *Moral Responsibility:* Individuals (or representatives of a company) seek to live their moral beliefs by doing the "right thing." The critical question is, "What do our moral beliefs and standards dictate that we should be doing?"

- *Social Responsibility:* Here, the objective is to be a good corporate citizen. Socially responsible managers want their corporations to act in ways that benefit society. The driving question is, "What do the best interests of society dictate that we should do?"

These several perspectives are all different, they are all equally legitimate. None is superior to another. In one way or other, they have inspired most of the current programs that organizations use to deal with the issues that tend to show up with work forces that are diverse. These programs cluster under two umbrellas: affirmative action and the "cultural awareness" programs collectively known as "valuing differences." We will consider these two in some detail in this chapter.

Very recently, a new perspective has been added to the list:

- *Management.* Here, managers place priority on the interests of their corporations. The principal questions are, "What do I as a manager need to do to ensure the effective and efficient utilization of employees in pursuit of the corporate mission?" and "What are the implications of diversity for how I manage?"

This *managerial* perspective is, of course, the focus of this book. It is an effort to call attention to a previously ignored approach that can enhance progress with both equal opportunity for employees and success for the corporation. It is also a move away from the historical assumption that the solution to diversity is assimilation.

Affirmative Action

Affirmative action has been the chief, often the exclusive, strategy for including and assimilating minorities and women into the corporate world. Sometimes companies were spurred by legal requirements, sometimes by moral beliefs, sometimes by a sense of social responsibility—or all three. Affirmative action programs grew out of a series of assumptions:

1. The mainstream in U.S. business is made up of white males.
2. Women and minorities are excluded from this mainstream because of widespread racial, ethnic, and sexual prejudices.
3. Such exclusion is unnecessary, given the strength of the U.S. economic edifice.
4. Furthermore, it is contrary to both good public policy and common decency.
5. Therefore, legal and social coercion are necessary to bring about change.

Three Affirmative Action Scenarios

Historically, affirmative action programs have taken one of three tracks: the passive, the pipeline, or the hierarchy approach.

Passive Scenario (Scenario 1). Corporate executives following this scenario take the necessary steps to ensure compliance with the law of the land. In particular, they take great pains to eliminate blatant expressions of discrimination and to educate their employees on what is acceptable behavior. The principal intervention here is affirmative action training for white males regarding racism and sexism.

Scenario 1 executives believe that achieving an environment free of blatant racism and sexism is synonymous with achieving equal opportunity. They reason that minorities and women now have an equal chance to join their corporations and to advance as far as their abilities can take them. When minorities and women fail to advance in the company, these managers blame poor preparation for corporate life. In their view, minorities will be able to take full advantage of corporate opportunities only after education systems have been improved.

Companies that take the passive approach resist initiating "special" efforts for women and minorities. They believe that such practices violate their concept of equal opportunity and constitute reverse discrimination and preferential treatment. They often speak of their desire to foster a "color-blind," "race-blind," and "gender-blind" environment.

Some companies in this passive scenario view affirmative action as good public relations. To enhance their image, these companies support organizations related to the "protected groups," offer scholarships and internships to minorities and women, advocate for minority and women's rights, and convey a posture of wishing to relate positively to women and minority communities. Indeed, a corporation can, through external affirmative action efforts, gain a reputation as a good place for women and minorities. However, such a reputation often belies the internal realities.

Pipeline Scenario (Scenario 2). Scenario 1 managers who become disillusioned with the intervention-free approach often move to the pipeline scenario. This approach continues legal obligations but goes beyond them to include motives of corporate social responsibility. Scenario 2 managers believe that social responsibility concerns justify interventions that increase the flow of quality minorities and women into corporate America.

These managers not only offer basic affirmative action training on racism and sexism, they prime the pipeline by encouraging minorities and women to enter occupations key to their corporation, and by creating or supporting "developmental" programs to enhance the assimilation of minorities and women. Their efforts result in a sizable number of minorities and women accepting entry-level positions.

Unfortunately, the upward mobility rates for the new entrants are still disappointing. Like Scenario 1 managers, Scenario 2 executives conclude that poor preparation is the major barrier to upward mobility. For them too, equal opportunity is a promise that minorities and women are ill-prepared to fulfill.

Upward Mobility Scenario (Scenario 3). Scenario 3 managers are motivated by moral considerations. Typically, they succeed in attracting "qualified" minorities and women to their corporations, achieve a level of comfort working with these employees, learn to respect their abilities—and become uncomfortable as they watch them cluster disproportionately at the bottom of the pyramid. Scenario 3 managers have experienced the competence of these individuals, and they're troubled by the unfairness of the situation. Reluctantly, they conclude that their corporation's systems are infected with institutionalized racism and sexism (a phrase that refers to those practices that are racist and sexist in effect, regardless of intent).

Yet rarely do they work to change the fundamental systems. Instead, they add to them with supplemental systems designed to contain the negative consequences. Mostly, they rely on further affirmative action efforts to forcibly break the ceiling. They provide "special" training activities aimed at minorities and women, set quantitative targets for the number of minorities and women to be developed and promoted, and set up mentoring programs and tracking systems.

Results can be encouraging. With commitment and persistence, managers can generate impressive upward mobility numbers.Yet Scenario 3 managers find themselves in a double bind. Their initiatives don't eliminate the ceiling. They simply generate temporary openings through which a limited number of women and minorities can advance. Maintenance of these gains requires an ongoing effort, for the pressures to move away from affirmative action are constant. Scenario 3 managers dare not relax—despite the growing dissatisfaction of minorities, women, and white males. They must continue the interventions to avoid losing past successes. They're caught in a frustrating cycle.

Similarities and Differences Among Scenarios. Major differences separate the three scenarios. Each assigns a different set of weights to legal, social responsibility, and moral motives. And they define equal opportunity differently. Scenario 1 and 2 managers think that they have achieved equal opportunity because they have attracted women and minorities at the entry level; scenario 3 companies want to see equal opportunity reflected in upward mobility rates. To that end, scenario 3 managers use affirmative action to foster upward mobility. Scenario 1 and 2 managers would view such a relationship as evidence of "reverse discrimination."

While the dynamics of the scenarios are distinct, the scenarios share similarities as well. Each, for example, sees assimilation as the ultimate goal. Scenario 1 managers assume that assimilation will occur on its own. Scenario 2 managers begin the assimilation process while prospective employees are still in the pipeline. Scenario 3 managers launch a number of explicit assimilation thrusts once minorities and women have joined the organization.

Similarly, managers in each scenario attribute the difficulties of minorities and women to inadequate preparation for corporate life. Scenario 3 managers often recognize the existence of institutionalized discrimination, but they typically focus their interventions on "better equipping" minorities and women to face this corporate reality.

Managers in each scenario are frustrated. The limitations of affirmative action have them puzzling over what they should do next in their pursuit of equal opportunity. Many wonder whether their equal employment opportunity and affirmative action goals are realistic. "Where," they ask, "do we go from here?"

The Limits of Affirmative Action

In one sense, affirmative action has produced results: large numbers of women and minorities are accepting entry-level positions in companies with strong recruitment efforts. But we must quickly add that these results are limited at best.

For one thing, minorities and women are disproportionately clustered at the bottom of the corporate pyramid. This phenomenon (called the glass ceiling when referring to women and premature plateauing when referring to minorities) exists even in organizations with excellent affirmative action reputations.

For another, there is the frustrating, and virtually unavoidable, affirmative action cycle. The traditional approach to diversity inevitably creates a cycle of crisis, problem recognition, action, great expectations, disappointment, dormancy, and renewed crisis (see Exhibit 2-1).

The cycle begins with recognition of a problem, a crisis: excessive turnover, inadequate upward mobility, or disproportionately low morale. Whatever the problem, the initial affirmative action remedy is recruitment, a frantic search to hire the "right kind" of person, whether it be a woman, a black, a Hispanic, or an Asian American. Affirmative action pictures the work force as a pipeline and reasons, "If we fill this pipeline with qualified minorities and women, we can solve our human resources prob-

Exhibit 2-1. The cycle stages.

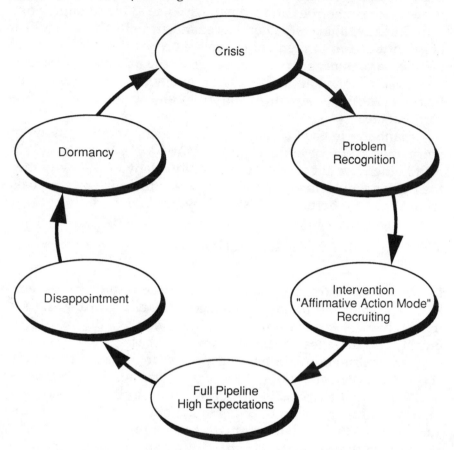

lem." "Qualified" translates to those individuals who are most likely to mesh with the corporation's current culture.

Following these recruitment periods, everyone experiences a period of high expectations. Unfortunately, however, hiring the "right" woman or minority doesn't necessarily solve the original problem. The newly hired employees don't progress as expected. White males complain about preferential treatment and reverse discrimination. Minorities and women are uncomfortably aware of the stigma of affirmative action activities.

Everybody's unhappy. Employees feel "stuck" and frustrated. Managers still have the original problem. In addition, they're not given credit for a good faith effort. Discouraged, they quit trying. At this point, the relaxation stage sets in. Affirmative action is placed on the back burner. This stage continues until the next crisis prompts action, and the cycle is repeated.

The Dynamics of Affirmative Action

Central to the problems associated with affirmative action is that it was never intended to be a permanent tool. Its intent was to fulfill a legal, moral, and social responsibility by initiating "special" efforts to ensure the creation of a diverse work force and encourage upward mobility for minorities and women. It was as if the government said to America's corporations:

> We have looked at the results of your people practices and they cause us to wonder about your commitment to equal opportunity. Further, we believe it will take considerable time for you to implement *corrective action* necessary for generating a *natural* capacity for bringing about the desired results. In the meantime, we will prescribe something that is artificial, transitional, and temporary: namely, affirmative action. It will give us relief from the negative consequences of your practices and give you time to take corrective action.

The problem is that managers have focused on affirmative action and ignored corrective action, assuming that the one *is* the other.

An example may help here. Corporation X's managers look at its development process and conclude that the system doesn't work as well for minorities and women as for white males. In an affirmative action mode, they establish a supplementary process for minorities and women. This process functions for two years and generates substantial gains in the development of the targeted groups.

At the end of two years, the company conducts a company-wide evaluation of its affirmative action program, and hears these assessments:

- *Minorities and Women:* "We applaud the objectives and the progress that has been achieved. But we regret the stigma attached to participating in a 'special' process. We recommend that everyone go through the regular system. Abolish the 'special' arrangement."
- *White Males:* "We applaud management's intent and the success that has been achieved. But frankly, we see the 'special' system as reverse discrimination and preferential treatment. We'd like to see everyone go through the regular system. Abolish the 'special' process."
- *Senior Management:* "It's obvious from our success that we now know how to manage minorities and women. Given this progress, we don't see the need to continue the 'special' process. Let's have everyone go through the regular system. Abolish the 'special' process."

The problem is that the "regular" system remains uncorrected. No one has asked why the system doesn't work *naturally* for everyone, what corrective actions might make it work naturally for all, or whether the existing culture will even allow the corrective action necessary to make the system work for everyone.

Given that the regular system has not changed, I predict that, should everyone go through it, the original conclusion will be affirmed, namely: "This system does not work well for minorities and women." I further predict that unless managers can expand upon the affirmative action mode, they will, upon reaching this conclusion, reestablish some version of the special process just abolished. And the cycle continues.

Valuing Differences

Organizations that have affirmative action programs in place often complement these efforts with various activities known collectively as valuing differences. They are designed to encourage awareness of and respect for diversity within the workplace.

Valuing differences programs are geared to the individual and interpersonal levels. The objective is to enhance interpersonal relationships among individuals and to minimize blatant expressions of racism and sexism.

Often valuing differences initiatives focus on the ways that men and women, or people of different races, reflect differences in values, attitudes, behavior styles, ways of thinking, and cultural background. These educational sessions can vary in length from one day (or less) to several days, or even occur on an ongoing basis. Some are confrontational, some nonconfrontational. They usually concentrate on one or several of these general objectives:

- Fostering awareness and acceptance of individual differences.
- Fostering greater understanding of the nature and dynamics of individual differences.
- Helping participants understand their own feelings and attitudes about people who are "different."
- Exploring how differences might be tapped as assets in the workplace.
- Enhancing work relations between people who are different.

Valuing differences programs can be thought of as derivative of affirmative action. With affirmative action, historically the assumption has been that dysfunctional behavior and attitudes can be attributed to malicious, deliberate decisions. Valuing differences assumes that undesirable behavior derives from a lack of awareness and understanding.

Companies where the quality of relationships among diverse employees is less than desired often find valuing differences thrusts attractive. In these situations, valuing differences can be very effective in enhancing relationships and minimizing blatant "isms." Companies with a strong moral perspective on diversity also find the valuing differences approach very appealing.

But acceptance, tolerance, and understanding of diversity are not by themselves enough to create an empowered work force. To empower a diverse group of employees to reach their full potential, managing diversity is needed.

Managing Diversity

Managing diversity doesn't seek to give relief from a system's negative consequences by adding on supplementary efforts. Instead, it begins with taking a hard look at the system and asking the questions that were not asked: Why doesn't the system work *naturally* for everyone? What has to be done to allow it to do so? Will the cultural roots of this company allow us to take the necessary corrective action? If not, what root changes do we have to make?

Stated differently, managing diversity begins with these fundamental questions: Given the competitive environment we face and the diverse work force we have, are we getting the highest productivity possible? Does our system work as smoothly as it could? Is morale as high as we would wish? And are those things as strong as they would be if all the people who worked here were the same sex and race and nationality and had the same lifestyle and value system and way of working? If the answers are no, then the solution is to substitute positive for negative aspects. That means *changing the system* and *modifying the core culture*.

Changing the root culture is at the heart of the managing diversity approach. Such an approach has a short-term drawback. It requires a considerably longer time frame than implementing an affirmative action initiative. Corporate cultures and systems don't change quickly. Managers in a pinch may find it appropriate to initiate an affirmative action process for short-term immediate relief while managing diversity is generating long-term changes.

Easing the Transition

Managing diversity is a new approach. That doesn't mean that it is entirely unrelated to or incompatible with other diversity approaches. It doesn't mean that the more traditional approaches aren't helpful. Managers who wish to have maximum options when dealing with employee diversity will want to use all three. Effectively doing so, however, requires a clear understanding of the action implications of each approach.

The following exercise offers you an opportunity to test your knowledge of the way in which the various approaches differ. Fourteen action scenarios are described here. Take a few minutes with each; then indicate whether the scenario represents an affirmative action, valuing differences, or managing diversity intervention. Use Exhibit 2-2 as a guide. If you have to make assumptions to make a judgment, please feel free to do so. The objective is not so much to come up with the "right" answer as it is to experience the logic and reasoning undergirding the three paradigms. The exercise will be most helpful if you delay reading the discussion following each scenario until you have reached a decision.

Scenario 1: A corporation establishes councils for each of the minority groups represented in its work force and also for women. This means that there are multicultural councils for blacks, Hispanics, Asian Americans, and white women. These councils serve as liaisons between management and the respective employee groups. Also, the councils function to provide support for individual members as they proceed with their careers in the company.

Discussion: You could argue that this is a valuing differences intervention, especially if you assumed that a significant reason for establishing the councils was to foster acceptance, tolerance, and understanding of minorities and women. If, however, you assumed that the critical reason behind establishing the councils was to create a liaison mechanism with senior management, this would be more of an affirmative action alternative. In the situation from which this scenario was drawn, the desire to improve relations between senior executives and minorities and women provided the principal motivation for creating the councils.

Scenario 2: A corporation provides a "learn the culture" training experience for its minority and women managers. In these seminars, participants explore the corporate culture's requirements for success. They develop strategies for enhancing their ability to conform with the prevailing culture.

Discussion: This is the prototypical assimilation program, and that makes this an affirmative action intervention. This program seeks to convey to minorities and women specifics about the

Exhibit 2-2. Affirmative action, valuing differences, and managing diversity—a comparative analysis.

Variables	Affirmative Action	Valuing Differences	Managing Diversity
Goal	Creation of diverse work force	Creation of diverse work force	Management of diverse work force
	Upward mobility for minorities and women	Establishment of quality interpersonal relationships	Full utilization of human resources
Motive (Primary)	Legal, moral and social responsibility	Exploitation of "richness" that can flow from diversity	Attainment of competitive advantage
Primary Focus	Acting affirmatively "Special" efforts	Understanding, respecting and valuing differences among various groups in the context of the business enterprise	Managing (creating an environment appropriate for full utilization of a diverse work force--emphasis on culture and systems.) Includes white males
Benefits (Primary)	-Creation of diverse work force -Upward mobility for minorities and women	-Mutual respect among groups -Creation of diverse work force -Upward mobility for minorities and women -Greater receptivity of affirmative action	-Enhanced overall management capability -Natural creation of diverse work force -Natural upward mobility for minorities and women -Competitive advantage for companies moving forward on the vanguard -Escape from frustrating cycle
Challenges	-Artificial -Creates own backlash -Requires continuous, intense commitment -Cyclical benefits	-Emphasis on interpersonal relations -Low emphasis on systems and culture -Low emphasis on "management" -Cyclical benefits	-Requires long-term commitment -Requires mindset shift -Requires modified definitions of leadership and management -Requires mutual adaptation by company and individual -Requires systems changes

corporation's culture and the requirements for conformity and as-similation. The message is, "If you wish to be successful, this is what you must do."

Scenario 3: A corporation holds multicultural days during which the respective cultures of the minority groups are featured. On Hispanic Day, for example, events highlighting various aspects of Hispanic culture are held, and the cafeteria features Hispanic food. Similar activities mark black and Asian American days.

Discussion: This "multicultural" activity aims to foster greater understanding of minorities and women. It is the prototype of valuing differences activities. This kind of intervention is popular, but its effectiveness varies. It is not uncommon for multicultural events to be supported primarily by members of the featured group, and thus the goal of enhanced understanding across groups is compromised.

Scenario 4: A company conducts research to identify issues with respect to minorities, white women, and white males. It then attempts to design strategies for addressing the issues that surfaced for each group. It also notes which issues are common to all groups.

Discussion: This is, in all probability, the beginning of a managing diversity approach. The tipoff is the inclusion of white males. Affirmative action and valuing differences interventions typically exclude this group.

Scenario 5: A corporation conducts training programs in which differences among the various groups—minorities, women, and white males—are examined as to their potential value for the business. Participants come away with an appreciation for both the differences that exist among employees and the ways in which these differences might contribute to the achievement of business objectives.

Discussion: We could argue that this is a valuing differences alternative if we assume that the objective is greater appreciation and understanding of differences and their relationships to business objectives. This argument is particularly valid if we assume that a critical driving objective is to help white males grow in their understanding of minorities and women rather than to help minorities and women understand white males.

A weaker (though plausible) argument could be made, however, that this intervention is somewhere between valuing differences and managing diversity. Here, we must assume that this step is intended to set the stage for managing diversity by facilitating an awareness of its business implications. The expectation would be that this greater awareness would encourage a willingness to learn how to manage diversity.

Scenario 6: A corporation appoints a "bridge the gap" task force to explore how more support personnel might make the transition to professional status. Secretaries, in particular, have been complaining that no matter how much experience or additional education they acquire, they remain secretaries.

Discussion: This is likely to be an affirmative action approach aimed at a kind of occupational classism. This task force typically will function as an appendage to the mainstream systems and culture and will generate stopgap measures. Fundamental change will not occur. This task force also could function in a valuing differences mode by encouraging greater understanding and appreciation of the support functions. Finally—an alternative that has not been commonly chosen—the task force could work for systemic and cultural change to facilitate movement across the gap. This would be in keeping with the managing diversity framework.

Scenario 7: A corporation conducts race relations seminars as a way of enhancing relationships among members of the different races represented in the work force. In these sessions, participants explore the nature of racism and the ways it might inhibit people's ability to reach their full potential.

Discussion: This is an interesting scenario. In the framework of the three approaches, this would be an affirmative action intervention. Indeed, it was a staple of affirmative action programs in the 1960s and 1970s.

We could also argue, however, that this is a valuing differences option intended to bring about greater acceptance, tolerance, and understanding of differences. Technically, this position stands up well. Conceptually, valuing differences assumes that lack of understanding, not racism or sexism, is the major challenge. Accordingly, prototypical valuing differences efforts focus on enhancing acceptance, tolerance, and understanding differences rather than on direct assaults on racism or sexism per se.

Scenario 8: For two years, senior managers of a corporation met to identify fast-trackers for line management. Early in the third year, one manager called "time out." He noted that every time a woman or a minority was discussed, the participants would raise objections. His question was, "Is this a real criterion operating or simply a lack of comfort with people who are different?"

Participants' first reaction was disbelief, but when they examined the records they concluded that the observation implicit in the question was accurate. They then set out to determine what factors were influencing their decisions.

Discussion: This reflects a managing diversity philosophy. In essence, the managers are asking, "Why doesn't this system work naturally for everyone?" Described here is an example of the kind of analysis of informal systems required by managing diversity.

Scenario 9: A corporation requires that leadership teams of its major divisions meet to explore how diversity might be a business issue for them. Once team members conclude that there are benefits to having a diverse work force and managing it effectively, they are helped to understand what managing diversity means and what initial "next steps" might make sense for them.

Discussion: This is the beginning of a managing diversity initiative. Essentially, the leadership teams are examining the importance of diversity to them. Presumably, if they conclude that it is a bottom-line issue, they will be motivated to explore managing diversity and its implementation requirements.

Scenario 10: A new CEO, distraught by the lack of progress his corporation has experienced with minorities and women, decrees that each major division will establish goals for the employment, promotion, and retention of these groups. He further de-crees that managers' performance evaluations and year-end bonuses will reflect the progress they have made in this area. As a result, affirmative action plans are developed and implemented. Within two years the number and distribution of minorities and women have improved significantly.

    Discussion: Represented here is a CEO's attempt to estab-lish an affirmative action program with accountability and re-wards. Results are achieved within the two-year time frame.

    Scenario 11: A corporation establishes a "work/family coor-dinator" position at each of its major facilities. The coordinators will assist employees to resolve conflicts at work and at home. Specifically, they will help employees take advantage of internal and external resources.

    Discussion: If the position is established to foster cultural and systemic change, it could be viewed as part of a managing diversity approach. But if it is merely a Band-Aid appendage, de-signed to minimize disruptions caused by work/family conflicts while leaving systems and culture intact, it represents probably a valuing differences approach. In reality, it might also reflect a modified affirmative action application.

    Scenario 12: In response to his affirmative action officer's de-scriptions of the difficulties being experienced with black males, a CEO replies, "Don't complicate things. Just go find qualified black males, hire them, and retain them. It's that simple. Do it." Within two years, the presence and involvement of black males at all levels increase markedly.

    Discussion: This affirmative action initiative aimed to rem-edy circumstances related to black males, and it worked. How-ever, when the sponsoring CEO departed, the results evaporated. Reportedly, most of the newly hired and promoted black males either stagnated, departed, or accepted demotions.

    Scenario 13: A CEO becomes convinced that culture is im-portant in creating an environment where affirmative action ini-tiatives can "take hold." He commissions a culture audit and uses the results as a basis for developing a plan for systematically modifying his corporation's culture. His goal: to develop a set of cultural assumptions that are congruent with what the company hopes to do with respect to minorities, women, and white males.

Discussion: The culture audit is at the heart of the managing diversity "way of life." The use of this audit and the inclusion of white males strongly imply that this is a managing diversity initiative.

Scenario 14: A corporation requires that all high-level managers become mentors/sponsors to high-potential women and minorities. It measures and rewards their performance on this task.

Discussion: Mentoring is a popular affirmative action intervention. The objective is to facilitate the assimilation of new hires. Although mentoring can in theory be a managing diversity mechanism that fosters shared adjustments by the new hire and the organization, mentoring in practice functions as an assimilation vehicle.

Looking Ahead

With these first two chapters, you have gained a general understanding of what the managing diversity approach is and how it relates to more familiar programs. In the next two chapters, you will see some of the pragmatic actions involved in initiating and implementing a managing diversity approach.

Chapter 3

Getting Ready for Change

"Your reasoning makes sense. But how do I make managing diversity concrete? Where do I begin? How do I move beyond theory?"

The questions are not surprising. The complexity of the managing diversity challenge and the magnitude of the task can make even the most enthusiastic change agents hesitate. Implementing a management approach to diversity involves a "way of life" change—a change of a corporation's roots. Changing a corporation's way of life is equivalent to changing an individual's personality. It does not come about easily. Matters are complicated further by the reality that most managers have limited knowledge of culture roots, let alone experience with changing them.

Those who wish to implement such a complex, long-term "life change" initiative must, first of all, be realists. They must understand the time, effort, commitment, and risk involved. They must also fully recognize the competitive and strategic imperatives driving the need for such change, and must have—or acquire—the skills to encourage "buy-in" from others. In this chapter, we begin to examine the elements of this extremely complex process. In the chapter that follows, we look at specific action steps.

The Complex Role of Change Agent

Managers who set out to implement change—particularly complex, long-term change—must start with themselves. Once they achieve maximum clarity about their personal vision and commitment, they can move on toward attempting to engage others in the task. We might think of these preliminary tasks as preparing the ground for planting.

Clarify Your Personal Vision. Managers have different visions of what they want to achieve through their diversity efforts. Some, like the senior manager who summed up a multiple-day session on diversity by noting how well participants had gotten along, want nothing more than peace. Others want to facilitate upward mobility for able employees, reduce turnover, take advantage of synergy, or increase morale. Still others seek strategic advantage, full utilization of human resources, enhanced capability of serving a diverse market, or an improved public image. These aspirations are appropriate and valid. But they can't be accomplished all at once. Potential change agents must clarify what they are hoping to achieve.

Furthermore, these managers can't think clearly about the future until they explore their current vision of diversity. One popular vision of diversity features minorities and women clustered on a relatively low plateau, with a few filtering up as they become assimilated into the corporate culture. Of course, this image includes good salaries and benefits and the expectation that financial rewards will make up for lack of upward mobility.

Another vision could be called "heightened sensitivity." Managers who hold this view are sensitive to the demands of minorities and women, and understand the advantages of helping them fulfill their potential. They envision minorities and women working at all levels of the corporation—but at their discretion. Minorities and women who advance in the corporation are perceived as being recipients of generosity. Employees who work for such a manager are aware of this. As a result, turnover is high, and those who stay aren't maximally productive.

Then there is the coexistence-compromise vision, held almost exclusively by white males. These managers agree that the interests of the corporation demand that they recognize minorities and women as equals. They bargain and negotiate their differences. But the win-lose aspect of the relationship maintains tensions, and the compromises reached are not necessarily to the company's competitive advantage.

Diversity and equal opportunity represent a quantum leap ahead. Managers who hold this vision are likely to be in a corporation where the formerly white male culture has been replaced by one more receptive to employee diversity. The problem is, however, that minorities and women accept this reality much more readily than do white males. As the formerly dominant cultural group, these men are likely to cling, consciously or unconsciously, to a vision that leaves them in the dominant position. The result is a "vision gap" between what the corporation's executives are aiming for and what many of their managers are able to reach.

For the aspiring change agent, the most useful vision is one that assumes a diverse work force and then says, "Let's create an environment that allows every single employee to do his or her best work."

Accept the Realities of Being a Change Agent. Managing diversity is not like a helium balloon; it will not fly on its own after being thrown into the air. This means that somebody must serve as drum major throughout the change process. This someone must be comfortable in front of, behind, on the side of, and even in the midst of the band. He or she must be willing, in short, to accept responsibility for ensuring that the band completes the planned march. In the absence of a champion, change seldom occurs.

The CEO of one corporation directed his managers to enhance the upward mobility of minorities and women. His subordinates responded to his directive by looking into managing diversity. But they were unprepared for the magnitude of change that managing diversity demands. One of the managers commented, "Our CEO only said he wants minorities and women to move up the pyramid. He didn't mention changing the organization's culture and systems or developing a new way of operating. How do we propose to convey to him the breadth of what we are now contemplating?" This manager was asking, of course, "Who cares enough to act as the change agent?" No one came forward. To this day, the corporation is involved in a series of disjointed stop-and-go approaches to diversity.

Clarify Motivation. Because the challenge is so enormous, the change agent absolutely has to have ample motivation to carry him or her through the process. Only the business rationale provides that motivation.

Clarify the Concepts. This is both critical and often ignored. Action-oriented managers, reluctant to spend the time to explore and understand concepts, often go forward without conceptual understanding. Given the complexity and comprehensiveness of managing diversity, action without conceptual clarity will hamper implementation.

Insist on Consistency. Language, as well as concepts, must be clearly understood and consistently used if managers and employees are to understand the managing diversity initiative. Within any one company, managers often use a wide variety of jargon about diversity and operate from a wide range of perspectives.

You might ask, "What difference does it make what you call it, as long as you *do* it?" The issue is the "it." Unless you take time to define "it" conceptually and insist on precision with terminology, you risk chaos. Individuals have agreed to do "it," but vastly different understandings of "it" guide their efforts. There is a great deal of bumping around.

The change agent, to facilitate the process, must insist upon consistency. Official definitions must serve as the point of departure for all change efforts. Do not, for example, use terms such as "multiculturalism," "pluralism," "valuing differences," "valuing diversity," "managing diversity," and "cultural diversity" as if they were all the same. Insist on a definition of terms and a consistency of use.

Foster a Pioneering Spirit. Going from New York City to Boston is a relatively risk-free activity—if you know that there are paved and well-marked roads connecting the cities. But if there are no roads—only wilderness—it's a very different trip, one characterized by risks, uncertainties, and serious challenges.

The managing diversity road to enhanced corporate competitiveness is in the process of construction. Managers desiring to advance this initiative must be able to tolerate challenge and ambiguity.

They also must be willing to help their people pioneer. Learning to manage diversity is a process, and one that is difficult at best. Corporate executives have the luxury of articulating a company policy. Middle managers, most of whom are still male and white—and very busy—have the responsibility for implementing it. When they succeed, it will be in small increments; when they fail, they'll be vulnerable to criticism. These managers need help; they need the change agent's support, and they need training. Most of all, they need recognition that theirs is a pioneering effort, that conflicts and failures come with the territory. Finally, they need to be judged accordingly.

Foster a Long-Term Perspective. Strategic change requires the perspective of the long-distance runner, not that of the sprinter. The change agent should do everything possible to encourage a long-term perspective. Celebrate small victories, take one day at a time, and hand over the baton carefully to the change agents who follow.

Conduct Diagnostic Research. This essential step is at the heart of the managing diversity approach. Its purpose is to identify the corporation's culture and systems and determine if they are supportive of managing diversity. This is a complex and time-consuming process, but a vital one. Because it is so central, it is discussed at length in the next chapter.

Emphasize Education Rather Than Training. Education has to do with how we think about things; training involves ways of doing things. Training builds specific skills; education changes mindsets. Major change efforts such as managing diversity require that people shift their mindsets, and that takes education. This education will be both ongoing and repetitive; people need to hear the message more than once. Change agents must educate *and* train.

Examples include the following:

▪ *One-on-one dialogues between the change agent and individuals affected by the proposed change.* Illustrative is the experience of one senior manager. This CEO had to delay change until he had sufficient time to educate his direct reports through an ongoing series of informal, one-on-one discussions. In these dialogues, the parties debated the pros and cons of a proposed major philosophical change. Once the direct reports' mindsets had shifted, they were able to proceed with planning the change.

- *One-on-one dialogues between a change agent and an outside consultant.* It is not uncommon for managers to remain flexible in their mindsets by continuing dialogues with individuals who have different perspectives.

- *"Stretching" seminars where participants are encouraged to think beyond their day-to-day operations and to explore new concepts.*

- *Attendance at professional societies' meetings.* Some professional societies have as one of their main objectives keeping their members abreast of new conceptual frameworks.

- *Workshops specifically designed to foster mindset shifts.* Here participants are introduced to alternative frameworks for a given issue and encouraged to explore implications for implementation and practice.

With "training," a key evaluative question is, "How will this experience improve my performance when I return to work?" With "education," it is sufficient to leave with "something to ponder" or "to chew on." Education, however, is an enabling activity. As the participants "chew," "ponder," and experience mindset shifts, they begin to see opportunities for application and change.

Involve Line Management. Implicit in the guidelines above is the involvement of line managers, but this is so important that it deserves explicit mention. The human resources department alone cannot drive managing diversity. Because managing diversity calls for significant change in the managerial practices of line managers, their buy-in is critical to successful implementation.

Continue Affirmative Action. The continuation of parallel—and vigorous—affirmative action, valuing differences, and traditional human resources programs will be essential for the foreseeable future. Managing diversity will require several years for its implementation, and many diversity-related issues will require immediate action. In the future, however, these alternatives will collapse into one more mature approaches capable of maximizing the contribution of all employees.

Emphasize the Interrelationships Between Managing Diversity and Other Ongoing Initiatives. The intent here is to help participants avoid overload. The change agent's job is to help managers and employees give meaning to all that is on their plate by helping them understand that it is all related and part of a comprehensive effort aimed at enhancing organizational performance.

Keep the Parallel Thrusts Distinct. While it is important to recognize interrelationships among various initiatives, it is also desirable to keep them distinct. Otherwise, embryonic efforts run the risk of being swallowed up by more mature initiatives.

Recruit Multiple Change Agents at All Levels. Successful implementation of managing diversity will require multiple change agents at all levels. Obviously, the CEO is in a position to exercise leverage as a change agent; however, others in the pyramid can also assume this role. Even when the CEO actively and vigorously functions as the change agent, successful implementation will require that others provide assistance throughout the hierarchy in making the change a reality.

For those who are at the middle and entry levels of the corporation, I am talking not about career-suicide but rather constructive and innovative initiatives based on an understanding of managing diversity and the dynamics of organizational change. These individuals in particular will need coaching as to how they can assume the change-agent role; otherwise, they are likely to think the risks of being proactive are too great.

Can implementation of managing diversity proceed without leadership from the CEO? If a manager or an organizational unit has a reasonable amount of autonomy and discretion, implementation without CEO leadership is possible *up to a point*. That point typically will be when a major cultural change is considered.

The change agent can be either a line or human resources manager. However, given the nature of managing diversity, implementation will be compromised greatly without the significant ownership and involvement of line management. Accordingly, if a human resources manager initiates implementation, a major challenge will be that of transferring ownership and leadership to line management. Human resources managers in most organizations are not likely to be able to foster managing diversity by themselves.

I have seen settings where human resources managers launch managing diversity and then work to secure line management ownership, where line managers are in the forefront, and where a combination of line and human resources managers provide leadership. Without a doubt, these experiences and the nature of managing diversity demonstrate that the involvement of line managers as change agents is absolutely critical.

One final note is in order. Although there may be a single champion of managing diversity, successful implementation will still require multiple change agents through the organization. Without multilevel change agents, implementation will be extremely difficult, if not impossible.

Overcoming Resistance

Even those courageous change agents who have taken the time to clarify their own vision and commitment and have worked hard to prepare the ground for a managing diversity initiative can encounter serious resistance from line managers, employees, even senior managers. This resistance springs from many sources.

Insufficient motivation. Most managers continue to see "diversity" as a legal, moral, or social responsibility rather than a business issue. As a result, diversity remains a "fair weather" agenda item—a luxury to be pursued when business results allow it and relegated to the back burner when sales or profits dip. Until managers perceive managing diversity as critical to the company's viability, they won't be sufficiently motivated to see implementation through.

The irony here is that some of the companies and managers who have the most difficulty with managing diversity are those who have been most vigorous in moving forward with affirmative action. Driven by legal, moral, or social responsibility motives, they resist viewing it as a business factor. As a result, those corporations most effective in creating a diverse work force may be at greatest risk in fully managing it.

Coping action: Care must be taken to foster an understanding of the business rationale for moving ahead with managing diversity. Managers must know how managing diversity can and will affect the viability of their departments and the entire organization.

Loyalty to assimilation. Some managers are so steeped in assimilation that they cannot imagine conditions under which employee diversity would be acceptable. They worry about what would happen if all employees "did their own thing." Other managers believe that the company's values are so appealing that few people could object to them; they can see no reason to reject assimilation.

Coping action: Educational interventions will be needed to wean managers away from overreliance on assimilation. This will be difficult, but it is doable. Individuals must be helped to explore ways of facilitating mutual adaptation on the part of the individual and the organization. Also, the change agent must help managers understand that the issue is not whether they like their company's values, but whether the values will help them manage an increasingly diverse work force.

Insufficient understanding of culture. Many managers have little understanding about corporate culture. For example, those who confuse roots with values are unlikely to be able to see the advantage of the managing diversity initiative.

Coping action: Again, education will be needed to help managers become comfortable with the concept of corporate culture and the mechanisms for building, changing, and maintaining it. Managers must come to see culture as one of their most effective tools for empowering employees. They must perceive culture to be tangible and meaningful, and within their span of influence.

Narrow definition of diversity. A significant inhibiting factor is the prevailing definition of diversity. By limiting the term to minorities and women, and ignoring diversity's other dimensions, this definition blocks understanding. It is extremely difficult, for example, for a white male who defines diversity in terms of minorities and women to stifle concerns about reverse discrimination and preferential treatment.

Coping action: This is tricky. The change agent must help people expand their definition of diversity to include more than race, gender, and ethnicity. However, at the same time, be careful not to overwhelm them with diversity's dimensions.

The "isms." Racism, sexism, and other "isms" still plague the workplace, and they keep people from fully accepting managing diversity. While the "isms" hinder advancing with managing diversity, they do not absolutely prevent progress. Managing diversity is possible, albeit difficult, in their presence.

Coping action: The "isms" should be addressed through ongoing valuing differences initiatives, with the intent of fostering understanding and acceptance of people who are different. This kind of initiative should minimize the "isms" and their impact as barriers.

Affirmative action baggage. In some situations, emotionalism and hard feelings related to affirmative action prevent rational consideration of managing diversity. Here, anything dealing implicitly or explicitly with race and gender issues is suspect. New approaches are viewed as efforts to sneak affirmative action in through the back door.

Coping action: Change agents must help managers and employees see that affirmative action, valuing differences, and managing diversity are not the same. Once people gain an appreciation of the differences and similarities among these three concepts, they should be less prone to assign affirmative action baggage to managing diversity.

Lack of strategic perspective. Individuals concerned with their corporation's need to stay ahead of the competition are quickest to embrace managing diversity, for the philosophy is more strategic than operational. In the absence of strategic thinking, corporate executives simply don't see the urgency of the initiative.

    Coping action: Managers who need to think strategically should be helped to differentiate between strategic thinking and operational/tactical thinking and planning. This requires both educational and training (skill building) efforts. These managers probably need a redefinition of their role as managers.

    Desire to avoid risk. Individuals who want to minimize risk prefer to stay clear of alternatives that have not been proved. They are uncomfortable with the uncertainties and ambiguities inherent in embryonic philosophies such as managing diversity. Because managing diversity is very much at the developmental/evolving stage, the fear of risk poses a major threat to implementation.

    Coping action: People seek to minimize risks for any number of reasons, some of which are personal and unique. Other reasons are grounded in organizational realities that discourage risk taking. The change agent's challenge is to work to eliminate all organizational aspects that discourage managers and employees from taking risks. Again, this may mean changing roots and modifying systems.

    Insufficient leadership. Only in the last decade or so have managers begun to perceive that management and leadership are not the same. Leadership involves ensuring that the organization has an appropriate vision, developing and articulating a strategy to gain competitive advantage, and building and maintaining a culture that support the vision and strategy. Because managing diversity is defined as a strategic tool, it will never be possible to implement it without leadership.

    Coping action: Managers must be helped to differentiate between leadership and management. They must come to realize that they are expected to both lead and manage in some combination. In sum, managers' understanding of what it means to be a manager must be redefined.

Managerial time frame. The attention span of most managers is relatively brief. Any change requiring more than two years is suspect as impractical. Fortunately, managers are becoming aware that not all issues can be packaged for their comfort.

Coping action: The more managers understand what empowerment management is and what it means to be a leader, the greater their understanding of the necessity for both a short-term and a long-term perspective.

Lack of power. Even when managers desire to move forward, they frequently don't have the power to proceed, or they don't have the know-how to expand their power base. So they become like cars that are mechanically sound, but immobilized by the lack of gasoline.

Coping action: The change agent has to sponsor some type of education program that will help managers become comfortable with the concept and acquisition of power. This means that managers must develop the skills to assess their power supply, understand the sources of this power, and develop mechanisms for replenishing it as needed. This is the essence of managing. For some managers, this attitude will be traumatic because they are accustomed to seeing power as negative. Change agents know that without power, managers can do nothing.

Inadequate change-management skills. Few managers possess skills or experience relevant to long-term change. They often start out well, but become frustrated and ineffective as the complexities, uncertainties, and ambiguities of long-term change take hold. This shortcoming can be a major obstacle even in the presence of good intentions and strong motivation.

Coping action: Managers who would be change agents must become familiar with the theory and practice of managing change. This means that in addition to being clear about managing diversity, valuing differences, and affirmative action initiatives, they must also be knowledgeable about and skilled in bringing about desired change.

Full plate. When hearing of the magnitude of effort required to implement managing diversity, managers frequently will complain that they don't have time for another major initiative. What they don't realize is that, implicitly or explicitly, most of what they must do requires managing diversity capability.

Coping action: The key here is to constantly relate managing diversity to other major initiatives under way. If this is not done, both managers and employees will become overwhelmed.

The Number-One Barrier to Acceptance

A major problem that change agents must overcome has to do with the way "managing" is defined in most corporations. Because this is such a significant barrier to acceptance of managing diversity, it warrants separate discussion.

In spite of recent trends toward participatory management styles, most managers in the trenches still believe in and practice the old top-down, directive style. They define "managing" as being a model, showing how the work should get done. Their "best" employees are those who come the closest to being clones of the boss.

They are what I call "doer" managers. For these managers, managing the business means *doing* the work. For an accounting manager, for example, this means practicing accounting. Doer managers make statements such as, "I wouldn't ask my people to do anything I wouldn't do myself; I roll up my sleeves and get in the trenches."

Doer managers perceive themselves as the center of the action—the "chief doer." They believe that the corporation values their abilities to *do* so much that other people have been assigned to them as a way of expanding their personal capability to perform. They believe, in other words, that employees are there to function as their extensions so that their ability to *do* is enlarged.

Doer managers see their job as two-dimensional: They must manage the business and manage people (see Exhibit 3-1). And they fail to integrate the two. Typically they talk of "people" and "business" issues as if they were unrelated. Furthermore, they see "doing" as their major task and taking care of people as secondary. They cherish the "real work" of doing (accounting, for example) and minimize the "managing people" activity. Any hint

Exhibit 3-1. Doer model.

of a "people challenge" is referred immediately to the human resources department.

When we look at the function of a manager this way, it's easy to see why the doer model is such a barrier to any attempt at managing diversity. First, it discourages acceptance of diversity. Doer managers seek people who can predictably clone their behavior. They aren't interested in the ways in which differences can enhance corporate profits. Second, doer managers don't see managing people as a legitimate activity. They will always have difficulty managing a diverse work force because they place no priority on managing people in general.

An alternative management style—and one more compatible with managing diversity—is the empowerment model (see Exhibit 3-2). This model defines the task of managing as enabling employees to behave in ways required to achieve business objectives. In this model, the duality between "business issues" and "people issues" is absent. Instead, the empowerment of employees is linked directly to or integrated with business objectives.

Under the empowerment model, managing is the priority, while doing is a secondary focus. Empowerment managers of accounting, for example, worry about whether they have done everything possible to fully enable accountants to do accounting. They're not concerned with doing the accounting themselves.

Facilitating Factors

Although the challenges are formidable, not all of the news is bad. Several factors combine to provide a receptive climate. Many

Exhibit 3-2. Empowerment model.

Manager ➤ Management Tools ➤ People ➤ Desired Behavior Patterns ➤ Business Objectives

of these we have already discussed, but in the context of getting your company ready for a change, they bear repeating.

- *Competitive realities.* Intense competition characterizes the international and domestic markets of the American corporation. This is a relatively recent development. Until the late 1970s and 1980s, American companies experienced substantial growth. Now, executives have to be on constant lookout for opportunities to gain competitive advantages. They cannot afford to bypass any good possibility.

- *Strategic realities.* Corporate leaders know that organizations that excel in tapping the potential of their people can gain a competitive edge. Few, however, have been willing to pay the price for gaining this advantage. As the work force becomes increasingly diverse and corporate environments more intensely competitive, the case for managing diversity will become clearer.

- *Limitations of affirmative action.* The negative feelings generated by affirmative action have resulted in a situation where this vehicle is more successful in maintaining previous gains than in producing additional breakthroughs. Even managers who are able to initiate successful affirmative action thrusts must deal with the backlash generated by both white males and some minorities and women. As a result, managers are looking for ways to complement their affirmative action efforts.

- *Legal, moral and social responsibility concerns.* These concerns lack the potency of the desire for competitive advantage. But they can help in generating a supportive climate for managing diversity.

- *Celebration of diversity.* Employees' attitudes are changing. They are more comfortable with being different and more reluctant to be assimilated. These developments invalidate the traditional assimilation approach to diversity and create the need for

an alternative. Managers who haven't come to grips with this issue will find themselves at a disadvantage as they compete with
those who have.

- *The absence of "neutral" diversity.* Many managers believe in-
tuitively that diversity is neutral, that if it is not leveraged as an
asset, it simply has no impact. Diversity in itself, however, is not
neutral. Whether diversity proves positive or negative will be a
function of the organizational environment, but in any event, it is
not neutral.

Without an environment that works well for all employees,
diversity works against you, simply because you do not have an
enabling context. It is only within the context of a supportive
managing diversity environment that unassimilated diversity becomes an asset and offers the opportunity to achieve a competitive gain; otherwise, it is a liability compromising organizational
effectiveness.

Chapter 4

Cultural Change: An Action Plan

Most corporate cultures were established when the vast majority of workers were white and male. Today's employees are more and more diverse. It's managerially prudent to ask if the culture that served you well in the past can serve you equally well in the present and the future.

But what if it doesn't? Suppose that question has been asked, and answered. Suppose that an astute observation of your business environment suggests that change is needed. Suppose, too, that a change agent has come forward and has begun to prepare the ground, using the ideas discussed in the last chapter. What next?

Sometimes executives who are introduced to a new idea decide it is the solution to all their problems and send their people scurrying in all directions with instructions to "do it"—whatever "it" is. Too often, the program takes off with a bang and then fades out with a whimper. This is particularly likely to happen with an initiative as complex and multifaceted as managing diversity. Successfully implementing this approach requires understanding the full process and designing an action plan that takes into account its many dimensions.

Identify Roots

The process of managing diversity begins with identifying the fundamental elements of the corporate culture, in particular those elements that influence or determine the company's philosophy about diversity. There is no substitute for this. Even though you may be sorely tempted to go straight to trying to change *how* people act, you cannot skip this investigation into *why* they act as they do.

Remember the organizational tree? Behavior that you see is a branch; the roots, the part you don't see, make the branch what it is. Managers who drive behavioral change on the assumption that the roots will follow are doomed to repeat the cycle.

Determining the nature of a company's roots requires research—what I call a culture audit. It is often conducted by an outside consultant, who is able to bring a degree of objectivity that is valuable in the diagnostic part of the research.

Through in-depth interviews, written surveys, reviews of relevant company documents (reports, manuals, memoranda), focus groups, and direct observations, researchers gather data on the company's many branches—the behaviors of managers and employees that relate to, or reflect, their attitudes toward diversity (see Appendix 4 for a generic set of interview questions). Depending on the trust level of the corporation, it is possible to use both insiders and outsiders to gather data.

The researchers' intent is to gather enough data about the branches to allow them to uncover the generating roots. This is a process of inference, and it typically is a joint effort between the consultants and a supporting group of the company's managers. What branches do we see? Therefore, what roots do we probably have?

Assess Roots

Once the roots have been identified, they must be examined as thoroughly as possible. The goal here is to determine whether they (and also the systems and practices they generate) support or hinder efforts to institute a management approach to diversity. This assessment is critical, since it provides the basis for planning change. The task here is to identify where change is needed— where a root may need to be removed or tweaked, and also where a root might be added.

This process of uncovering and evaluating roots may become clearer if we consider a few examples. One common root, for example, is the "melting pot" mythology. This root is manifested in the organization that prides itself on being "color-blind." People in this organization say, "It doesn't matter where you came from as long as you fit in." The implications? This company expects everyone to assimilate. Diversity is unacceptable.

Still another root assumption is that "cream rises to the top." This assumption ignores the reality that in most companies, cream is pulled or pushed to the top by an informal system of mentoring and sponsorship. The implications? To get the best from a diverse work force, the mentors and sponsors must work effectively for all groups.

Here's another: "This company is like a family." That root is extremely common—and extremely destructive. A major manifestation is a paternalistic climate where managers take on parental roles and employees are seen much like children. Inherent in this scenario is that "father (the boss) knows best" and children (employees) should follow his example. Implicit also is that sons will inherit the business, daughters should stick to doing the company dishes, and Uncle Deadwood deserves to stay around regardless of his performance.

The implications? Success in paternalistic companies is defined by how closely people emulate the manager. Taken to the extreme, this scenario aspires to have every single employee be a clone of the boss. This is the very opposite of diversity.

Flowing from the "family" root in some corporations is a rigid definition of loyalty as childlike obedience and emulation. Employees are expected to obey the manager; in return, they expect that this behavior will eventually be rewarded. For example, in one company managers expected employees to relocate as often and as quickly as necessary —regardless of their personal circumstances. To do otherwise was to risk being labeled disloyal.

Another example of this loyalty expectation is the executive who long ago set up a pattern of coming to work early and leaving late. It's unspoken, of course, but the expectation is that everyone else will do the same. Now he stands at his window, monitoring employee arrivals and departures. Failure to adhere to his personal pattern is viewed as disloyalty.

As the work force becomes more diverse with employees having needs and preferences unlike their bosses, managers desiring to create a facilitative environment will have to redefine loyalty.

Another culture root that is becoming common is, "We are all a team." In many ways this root supports diversity—certainly more effectively than "family" cultures—but there can be difficulties with it as well. The problem has to do with the style of developing, nurturing, that works best for various employees.

The "team" assumption often generates a rough-and-tumble, athletic kind of nurturing—much as a sparring partner prepares a boxer for a fight, or the second-string football team pushes the first string. This works well for some, but not all.

In a rap session between a CEO and a group of employees, one person complained that the corporation's environment was not a nurturing one. He spoke of the challenging, argumentative tone of meetings and boss-subordinate exchanges that he frequently observed. The CEO was surprised; he considered the athletic-type behavior very supportive and facilitative. For this employee and others of similar mind, the corporation's development process was sorely lacking.

Identify and Plan for Root Changes

To this point, we have unearthed the core cultural assumptions, or roots, that determine a company's behavior with respect to diversity issues, and we have analyzed the impact of those cultural roots on the success of a managing diversity approach. Quite an accomplishment. Now the task is to identify what roots need to be changed, and in which direction. To do that, we contrast the current roots with the desired roots. Again using the "family" root as an example, the change agent must determine, "If we are not family, what are we? What should we be?"

Once the needed changes have been identified, then we move on to determine how to move from the status quo to the desired root. The manager driving the root modification—the change agent—must develop a full-scale plan for deliberately and definitively bringing about the change. Changing roots requires direct and straightforward action steps, as opposed to indirect approaches.

Work on the root level is laborious. For every root, there are many branches, multiple corporate decisions and actions, and each one has its constituencies. Be prepared for opposition. Deeply entrenched roots have developed some powerful defenders. Whenever these "root guards" hear the words "change" and "roots" in the same sentence, they snap to attention and ask in unison, "What root do you propose to change?" If you tell Uncle Deadwood, for example, that "we think it's time that you produce or move on," shock waves will travel through the company. Family-oriented employees will rush to defend the sacred concept of loyalty.

Root guards, in their efforts to discourage arbitrary root change, will sometimes try to inflict pain. If you endure the pain and still see the need for root change, however, the guards will usually grant you a hearing, especially if you convince them of the urgency with a firm business rationale. Maybe your business environment has changed so drastically that success depends on new branches that are incongruent with the existing roots. Root guards are most receptive to root changes once they understand that the risks of inertia outweigh the risks of changing.

Corporate root change is not for the squeamish. Yet managers committed to equal opportunity for all employees must exert the effort. The reward is a strategic advantage over the competition.

Root Change: An Example

Cultural investigations can take on particular poignancy in the case of a merger or an acquisition. The cultural roots and manifestations of the "acquirees" are especially vulnerable, but even the friendliest of mergers can also create cultural clashes and the necessity for root changes. To see this challenge from a managing diversity perspective is to determine which roots will control the vision of the new combined entity. How can, or should, the two roots systems be meshed and integrated?

In an acquisition, often the roots of the acquiring company

remain dominant, and those of the acquiree are assimilated; we might call this the *branch* approach. The acquirer treats the acquiree as though it had no roots, as though it were solely a collection of branches. The acquiree's branches are dismembered and attached to the "main" company's trunk. The acquiring company's managers expect "acquiree" employees to "fall into line" almost automatically.

This approach works well if the roots of the two companies are similar. If the roots are dissimilar, however, the attached branches are destined to wither, die, and fall off. Remember my peach limb?

If the acquiring company recognizes the existence of the acquiree's culture but still believes its own should be dominant, we would expect to see the *acculturation* approach. Here the acquiring company undertakes intense socialization to bring about integration. Even though this is different from the branch approach, the result is the same—the acquired company adopts the acquiring company's way of doing business.

Another option is *reverse acculturation*, in which the roots of the acquired company infiltrate and modify the roots of the acquirer. Essentially, the acquiring corporation sees the acquisition as an intervention to bring about change in its own roots. This approach, too, relies on assimilation.

A fourth option, however—the *hybrid* option—calls for managing diversity. Here the acquiring managers would seek to build a new culture reflecting the strong points of both organizations' root systems. This is a long-term process requiring both vision and considerable leadership skills.

The hybrid option would, for example, require an acknowledgment that the two cultures differ and an "up front" decision on which aspects of each culture are most valued. It would also require that the agreed-upon vision be made clear to both managers and employees, and that it become the driving force for managers in both companies.

Senior managers pursuing a hybrid vision must foster problem-solving and conflict-resolution capability; this probably calls for special training sessions. Under the hybrid vision, the issue of "who bought whom" would become less important than the issue of how to bring about the desired hybrid culture.

Growing New Roots

- *Repeatedly articulate new roots.* One of the first steps in moving toward the new set of roots is to articulate them repeatedly. One organizational participant said of a corporate leader, "He says the same thing over and over—when you join the organization, at the anniversary of your joining, at celebrations of performance, at retirement parties, at planning sessions—whenever. He looks for opportunities to deliver the same message."

Granted, employees and managers may find this boring. But repetition continually reaffirms the roots as drivers and determinants of behavior. In the absence of such reaffirmation, employee behavior is increasingly likely to fall outside acceptable limits.

- *Create supportive traditions and ceremonies.* Every corporation has traditions and ceremonies: orientation programs, promotion and retirement parties, annual employee meetings, company picnics, and the like. The cultural change agent must examine these to ensure that they fit with the root change and to see how they might serve as levers for facilitating implementation. For example, check the orientation program for new employees; does it incorporate concepts and principles conducive to managing diversity?

- *Create appropriate heroes and heroines.* Managers can also support desired root change by choosing carefully whom they raise as heroes. A CEO pushing empowerment management, for example, would not want to foster the recognition of doer managers as heroes. Instead, she would award hero or heroine status to empowering managers, those who put priority on managing people as the principal means of achieving business objectives.

- *Create supportive symbols.* In organizations, symbols take on a reality beyond the literal meaning of their nature. For example, in one corporation all new employees assembled for orientation around a table built by the company founders. The table became a symbol of the roots put in place by the founders. Gathering around the table symbolized the expectation that newcomers would align themselves with the existing corporate culture. A change agent would work to ensure that this assimilation expectation was supportive of the new roots.

- *Influence communications networks.* Change agents need to influence both the corporation's formal and informal communications networks. They must be willing to use storytellers and whisperers (spreaders of rumors), as well as formal policies, manuals, reports, and memoranda, in pursuit of cultural change. Otherwise, they risk the possibility that informal communication networks will work against them. A few moments with a gossip and a few well-placed stories with effective storytellers can help enormously with the development of an overall climate facilitative of the new root.

- *Recruit new root guards.* Because new roots are fragile, guards must be enlisted to protect them from old root guards. These recruits will not only protect the embryonic roots but accept responsibility for nurturing them as well. Change agents who don't deal with this recruitment task may find that their hard-earned changes are short-lived.

Essentially, the recruitment task involves identifying and educating those who are predisposed toward the change. They will then become root guards for the new roots. Managers aware of the limitations of the family root, for example, would be prime candidates for guarding the new roots.

- *Reward change agents.* Changing and maintaining corporate culture as opposed to operating within a given set of roots is a leadership task. Yet, unfortunately, corporate practices often don't encourage and reward this type of leadership behavior. Instead, they emphasize short-term operational achievements. Successful cultural change efforts will require a shift in priorities so that change agents are encouraged to work on changing culture and to persevere over the long run.

Change the Systems

A tree behaves the way it does—produces holly berries or acorns, has yellow flowers or no flowers, drops its leaves in autumn or remains evergreen—because of its roots. In organizations, the roots determine how things work in that organization, how managers do their job, how employees are treated; in other words, all the behaviors that collectively characterize the company.

These behaviors constitute the corporation's systems, both formal and informal. This is where things get tangible: the systems determine employees' future in the organization. The most important reason for examining and modifying cultural roots is to enable meaningful, sustainable modification of systems. The type of analysis conducted on the corporation's culture must be carried out for its systems as well. In essence, the task here is to look hard at all your systems and determine whether they help foster a managing diversity approach or hinder it. Stated differently, the diversity change agent must ensure that organizational systems affirm the new roots.

One very important example is the way people are developed for greater responsibility: the system of promotions, mentoring, and sponsorship. In many organizations, for example, it is difficult to secure a promotion above a certain level without a personal advocate or sponsor. In the context of managing diversity, the issue is not whether this system is maximally efficient but whether it works for all employees. Executives who sponsor only people like themselves are not making a contribution toward managing diversity.

Performance appraisal is another significant system. If left unexamined, practices within this system can have devastating effects. There are, for example, organizations where official performance appraisals have little in common with what is said informally in the executive lounge. Minorities and women operating within this system seldom get accurate appraisals of their performance, and so it is difficult for them to correct or defend their alleged shortcomings.

Consider the reward system. If managing diversity is to become a reality, the system must reward empowering managers and make sure *not* to reward doer managers. The objective is to avoid giving off conflicting signals: championing one behavior while rewarding another.

In the case of the hybrid culture being developed by acquiring and acquiree companies, sensitive managers will take great care to require that all the "people" systems of the combined company—rewards, measurement, education, development—reflect the new vision.

Settle In for the Long Haul

Culture change is a long-term process. It takes years, for example, just to establish supportive traditions. One corporation that has been implementing managing diversity for roughly four years has made only limited progress in bringing about the necessary mind-set shifts.

We are talking about a relatively new phenomenon, and there is little accumulated experience to help us know what is a "typical" time frame. However, I believe that fifteen or twenty years of consistent and conscientious efforts will be required before a cultural change becomes naturally sustainable. Both managers and employees need to know this. In the meantime, the process of diagnosis, planning, intervention, monitoring, and evaluation must be ongoing. Reaching the desired end requires that we keep note of where we are going.

Appendix 4
The Culture Audit

The questions below are administered, either through in-depth interviews or written survey instruments, to roughly 20 percent of the total population of the organization. Why 20 percent? The goal is to continue gathering data until there is redundancy, which can happen at around 7 or 8 percent, to sample enough participants so that a broad sense of ownership of the data is generated, and to protect confidentiality of minorities and women by oversampling where their numbers are relatively few. The interview is often administered by an outside consultant to ensure objectivity and confidentiality.

Once completed, interview schedules are coded for computer input and frequency tables are developed. These frequency data, in turn, become a principal basis for developing conclusions and recommendations.

INTERVIEW GUIDE

The purpose of this interview is to help us understand how you and other employees feel about working at the ORGANIZATION NAME so that we can make suggestions that can improve the work environment. Please answer each question as completely as possible. This questionnaire will be used only by the consultants, and your individual answers will be held in strict confidence. No one will be individually identified in our report. So please feel free to tell us anything you think we may need to know.

_____ Interviewer

1. Are you _____ Hispanic

   _____ Asian American

   _____ American Indian

   _____ White

   _____ Black

   _____ Other (Please specify: _____)

2. Are you _____ Female or _____ Male?

3. How long have you been with the ORGANIZATION NAME?

   _____ 1 year or less

   _____ Over 1 year, but less than 3 years

   _____ 3 to 5 years

   _____ 6 to 10 years

   _____ 11 to 20 years

   _____ Over 20 years

4. Is your present position:

   _____ Supervisory

   _____ Nonsupervisory

5. What is your title and function?

6. Since coming to work at the ORGANIZATION NAME, have you received any promotions? That is, have you been given more responsibility *and* a pay increase that went along with taking more responsibility?

   _____ Yes

   _____ No

7. Which of the following best describes your level of education when you joined the ORGANIZATION NAME?

   _____ Did not graduate high school

   _____ High school graduate or GED

   _____ Some college, vocational, or technical training beyond high school

   _____ Associate's degree

   _____ Bachelor's degree

   _____ Master's degree

   _____ Doctorate or professional degree

8. Have you continued or completed any educational degree programs since joining the ORGANIZATION NAME?

   _____ Yes

   _____ No

9. Over the time that you have been with the ORGANIZATION NAME, what are some of the major changes you have seen? (Examples would include organizational changes, changes in policies or procedures, technology, types of clients, or benefits to employees.)

10. What makes the ORGANIZATION NAME good at what it does?

11. What attracted you to the ORGANIZATION NAME?

12. On a scale of 1 to 10, with 1 representing "mostly *unfulfilled*" and 10 representing "mostly fulfilled," please rate the extent that

your expectations have been met at the ORGANIZATION NAME. (Please circle the most appropriate rating.)

MOSTLY   MOSTLY
UNFULFILLED   1   2   3   4   5   6   7   8   9   10   FULFILLED

13. What have been the most important sources of fulfillment of your expectations?

14. What have been the most important reasons for your sense of unmet expectations, or frustrations?

15. What kinds of things have encouraged you to stay with the ORGANIZATION NAME?

16. Have you ever seriously thought about leaving the ORGANIZATION NAME?

    _____ Yes (Continue with #17)

    _____ No (Go to #18)

17. What was going on at that time that made you consider leaving?

18. Given your experiences to date, if you were going to hire someone to do the kind of work that you do, what kind of person would you hire?

19. What is required to be successful at the ORGANIZATION NAME?

20. Do you consider yourself successful here at the ORGANIZATION NAME?

    _____ Yes (Continue with #21)

    _____ No (Go to #22)

    _____ Don't Know (Go to #23)

21. If yes, what two or three experiences have contributed to your success?

22. If no, why do you think of yourself as unsuccessful?

23. What kind of formal training programs have you attended since coming to the ORGANIZATION NAME? (If you have attended more than three, check the three in which you have had the most training.)

24. Was this training (please check one):

        _____ Requested by you?

        _____ Recommended by your supervisor?

        _____ Required?

        _____ A combination of the above?

25. Have you received any on-the-job training?

        _____ Yes (Continue with #26)

        _____ No (Go to #27)

26. How would you rate the on-the-job training you have had?

        _____ Excellent

        _____ Good

        _____ Average

        _____ Fair

        _____ Poor

27. During your career here at the ORGANIZATION NAME, have you had a mentor, coach, or someone especially interested in you to help you with your job?

        _____ Yes (Continue with #28)

        _____ No (Go to #31)

28. How many mentors or coaches have you had at the ORGANI-ZATION NAME?

29. How did this (these) relationship(s) come about? (Please check one.)

        _____ I asked for help.

        _____ Supervisor offered help.

        _____ Coworker offered help.

        _____ Supervisor and coworker offered help.

        _____ Friend/family member helped.

        _____ Other (Please specify:_____)

30. How would you describe your experiences with your mentor(s)?
    Would you say they have been:

    _____ Damaging to your career

    _____ Not helpful

    _____ Helped a little

    _____ Somewhat helpful

    _____ Very helpful

31. Have you ever been, or are you presently, a mentor or a coach
    for another employee at the ORGANIZATION NAME?

    _____ Yes (Continue with #32)

    _____ No (Go to #35)

32. How many people at ORGANIZATION NAME have you men-
    tored or coached?

33. How did this (these) relationship(s) come about? (Please check
    one.)

    _____ They asked for help.

    _____ I was their supervisor.

    _____ They were (a) coworker(s).

    _____ They were coworkers and employees.

    _____ They were friends/relatives.

    _____ Other (Please specify: _____)

34. How would you describe your experiences as a mentor?

    _____ Very *un*rewarding

    _____ *Un*rewarding

    _____ Sometimes *un*rewarding, sometimes re-
                warding

    _____ Rewarding

    _____ Very rewarding

35. Is there anything that keeps you from contributing all that you can to your job?

    _____ Yes (Continue with #36)

    _____ No (Go to #37)

36. What are some of the things that prevent you from contributing?

37. To be successful in your work, are there any *unwritten* rules that you are expected to follow?

    _____ Yes (Continue with #38)

    _____ No (Go to #39)

38. What are some of these unwritten rules?

39. Do you get informal feedback about how you are doing on the job?

    _____ Yes (Continue with #40)

    _____ No (Go to #41)

40. How useful is this informal feedback to you in the performance of your job?

    _____ Not useful

    _____ Barely useful

    _____ Somewhat useful

    _____ Mostly useful

    _____ Very useful

41. How often do you receive a formal performance review (or evaluation)?

    _____ Quarterly (every three months)

    _____ Semiannually (every six months)

    _____ Annually (once a year)

    _____ Sporadically

    _____ Never (Go to #43)

42. How useful is this formal performance review to you in the per-
    formance of your job?

    _____ Not useful

    _____ Barely useful

    _____ Of some use

    _____ Mostly useful

    _____ Very useful

43. Thinking about all the supervision that you have had since join-
    ing the ORGANIZATION NAME, please rate the *overall* quality
    of supervision that you have had at the ORGANIZATION NAME
    on a scale from 1, which would be the worst rating, to 10, which
    would be the best rating. (Please circle the most appropriate rat-
    ing.)

    WORST   1   2   3   4   5   6   7   8   9   10   BEST

44. What have been some of the most important *positive* aspects of
    the *overall* supervisory attention you have received since joining
    the ORGANIZATION NAME?

45. What have been some of the most important *negative* aspects of
    the *overall* supervisory attention you have received since joining
    the ORGANIZATION NAME?

46. Thinking now about the quality of supervision that your *current*
    supervisor has provided, please rate the overall quality of the
    current supervision that you are receiving on a scale from 1,
    which would be the worst rating, to 10, which would be the best
    rating. (Please circle the most appropriate rating.)

    WORST   1   2   3   4   5   6   7   8   9   10   BEST

47. What have been some of the most important *positive* aspects of
    the *current* supervision you are receiving?

48. What have been some of the most important *negative* aspects of
    the *current* supervision you are receiving?

49. On a scale from 1 to 10, with 1 representing the worst rating and
    10 representing the best rating, please rate the overall quality of
    career development attention that supervisors have provided you

at the ORGANIZATION NAME. (Please circle the most appropriate rating.)

WORST   1   2   3   4   5   6   7   8   9   10   BEST

50. What have been the *positive* aspects of the career development attention that you have received at the ORGANIZATION NAME?

51. What have been the *weaknesses* of the career development attention you have received at the ORGANIZATION NAME?

52. When you have a problem that you believe needs to be addressed, do you feel that you are able to bring it up with your current supervisor?

    _____   Yes, for all problems (Go to #54)

    _____   Yes, for most problems (Go to #54)

    _____   Yes, for some problems (Continue with #53)

    _____   No, never (Continue with #53)

53. Why don't you feel that you can discuss problems with your current supervisor?

54. What does the ORGANIZATION NAME do to help its supervisors do the best possible job?

55. What does your immediate management do when something goes *wrong*?

56. What does your immediate management do when something goes really *well*?

57. What does your immediate management really pay attention to?

58. In the context of performance appraisal, do you think managers at the ORGANIZATION NAME are rewarded on the basis of employee development?

    _____   Yes (Continue with #59)

    _____   No (Go to #60)

59. If yes, what are the most important rewards that managers get for people development?

60. To what extent does your manager's evaluation of your work influence your own assessment of your work?

_____ None

_____ A little

_____ Some

_____ A great deal

_____ Totally

61. On a scale of 1 to 10, with 1 representing the worst rating and 10 representing the best rating, please rate how the ORGANIZATION NAME is doing in using the different talents of all its people. (Please circle the most appropriate rating.)

WORST   1   2   3   4   5   6   7   8   9   10   BEST

62. What, if anything, needs to be done to help minorities to do their jobs better and advance at the ORGANIZATION NAME?

63. What, if anything, needs to be done to help women to do their jobs better and advance at the ORGANIZATION NAME?

64. What, if anything, needs to be done to help office personnel to do their jobs better and advance at the ORGANIZATION NAME?

65. What, if anything, needs to be done to help white males to do their jobs better and advance at the ORGANIZATION NAME?

66. Is it acceptable for you to discuss with your supervisor issues of racism, sexism, or other biases held by other employees?

_____ Yes (Go to #68)

_____ No (Continue with #67)

67. Why is it not acceptable for you to discuss these issues? (Go to #69)

68. What are some examples of issues you have discussed with your current supervisor?

69. How optimistic (positive) or pessimistic (negative) are you about progress being made at the ORGANIZATION NAME in providing equal opportunity for all employees?

_____ Very pessimistic (Continue with #70)

_____ Somewhat pessimistic (Continue with #70)

_____ Neither optimistic nor pessimistic (Go to #72)

_____ Somewhat optimistic (Go to #71)

_____ Very optimistic (Go to #71)

70. Please describe the reasons for your *negative* reaction.

71. Please describe the reasons for your *positive* reaction.

72. On a scale from 1 to 10, with 1 representing the worst and 10 representing the best, please rate the *quality of worklife* at the ORGANIZATION NAME. (Please circle the most appropriate rating.)

WORST   1   2   3   4   5   6   7   8   9   10   BEST

73. On a scale from 1 to 10, with 1 representing the least effective teamwork and 10 representing the most effective teamwork, please rate the *degree to which you feel that you are an effective member of a team* at the ORGANIZATION NAME. (Please circle the most appropriate rating.)

LEAST   MOST
EFFECTIVE   1   2   3   4   5   6   7   8   9   10   EFFECTIVE

74. On a scale of 1 to 10, with 1 representing the lowest respect and 10 representing the highest respect, please rate the *degree to which you feel that you are treated with respect* at the ORGANIZATION NAME. (Please circle the most appropriate rating.)

LOWEST   HIGHEST
RESPECT   1   2   3   4   5   6   7   8   9   10   RESPECT

75. In general, what is the future of the ORGANIZATION NAME as an organization?

_____ Poor

_____ Fair

_____ Good

_____ Excellent

76. Finally, thinking back over the things we have talked about, do you think that most of your coworkers here would look at these issues the way you do?

    _____   Yes

    _____   No

    _____   Don't know

THANK YOU FOR YOUR HELP

Should you have any additional comments, please use the space below to provide them.

Chapter 5

"What If?" A Report on the Ideal

A number of pioneering organizations have taken significant steps toward managing diversity, but no one company has moved to the point where managing diversity is a full reality. We cannot point to any one corporation as a model for complete implementation of managing diversity. Still, the questions persist: "How do I do it? How do I move from theory to concrete reality?"

This chapter illustrates how the model presented in Chapter 4 might play itself out operationally. In a composite case history based on several real situations, we will watch a hypothetical company as it institutes a managing diversity process over a period of five years.

Compound Products, Inc.: 1991

Compound Products produces aluminum and plastic products for retail and commercial markets (in its Aluminum Division) and aluminum and plastic components for scientific and governmental use (the Scientific Components Division). The company also operates a state-of-the-art research center with several regional facilities that specializes in developing new applications for aluminum and plastics; indeed, most of the company's growth over the past ten years has come through the work of the research center.

Met City Plant

The plant at Metropolitan City (Met City) is approximately twenty-five years old; it is a flagship manufacturing facility for Compound. Its vibrancy and history of good performance have allowed it to play a central role both regionally and nationally.

The plant, strategically located in a southern valley of a southeastern state, furnishes the region with aluminum and plastic products. Also on the plant site is a regional research center. (The research function was decentralized as a way to foster interaction with the manufacturing operations.)

The plant has 4,050 employees—about 1,200 in each division and the remainder in the regional research center. Of the total population, 91 percent are in managerial, professional, or skilled labor slots; only 9 percent are engaged in low-skill activities.

Although a few minorities and women are middle-level managers and professionals, most are at lower- and entry-level slots. Isolated instances of minorities and women moving to upper-middle levels could be cited over the past twenty years, but these employees left Compound relatively quickly. Recently, the plant manager, Bob Walker, indicated a strong desire to enhance upward mobility for minorities and women at the plant.

Affirmative Action at Met City

At Met City and other locations, Compound enjoys an outstanding reputation in the affirmative action arena. Human resources managers at other Met City companies consistently give the annual Affirmative Action Pacesetter award to Compound Products. The company's senior managers traditionally have been committed to hiring minorities and women. Initially, this meant a significant presence of blacks and women; however, as Hispanics and Asian Americans have become more numerous at Met City, their employment at the plant has been on the rise. Asian Americans, in particular, are concentrated at entry and low levels in the research center's professional ranks, where they have earned reputations for being intelligent and industrious.

Currently, the employee population is: white males, 40 percent; white females, 28 percent; blacks, 21 percent; Hispanics, 7 percent; and Asian Americans, 4 percent.

In addition to aggressively hiring minorities and women, the Met City plant has offered all employees at least one day of sensitivity training on race and gender issues. In fact, the plant has provided three waves of this training, so long-term employees have experienced three of these sessions. Sam Jones, affirmative action director at Met City, is troubled because the training doesn't seem to "take."

> No matter how well the training goes, we always seem to need a refresher course. Racial and sexual incidents persist. They wane immediately after training, only to return later.

Even more troubling for Sam, the plant has not been able to establish a cadre of minority and women managers among its upper-middle ranks:

> About eight years ago, we intentionally promoted women and blacks to significant upper-middle positions. The result was subtle, but effective, backlash. More than half of these promotees were charged with incompetence, while the remainder were harassed in a variety of ways. All have left the company. Some reportedly moved on to greener pastures; at least that's the public story. The reality is that all left discontented.

Other Met City affirmative action thrusts have included outreach efforts with the local schools; internships for minorities and women; support of local initiatives undertaken by the United Negro College Fund, the Urban League, and the National Association for the Advancement of Colored People; and contributions to various scholarship programs for minorities and women.

The General Manager's Agenda

Bob Walker, who became plant manager three years ago, has continued to build on the plant's successes. Profitability, productivity, and quality have all improved significantly since he assumed the position. Given his record of accomplishment at smaller Compound plants, his progress has been no surprise.

Sam has been watching Bob's moves with interest, and feels that he will eventually focus on affirmative action. Bob has said all the right things but has not demanded specific results. About six months ago, however, he called Sam into his office:

> Sam, I've been here for roughly three years, and from what I can tell, the plant is resting on its past laurels as far as affirmative action is concerned. Clearly, we've done some good things in the past, but they have not stuck. It's criminal that we do not have women or minorities among the plant's senior managers, nor do we have anyone near being ready.
>
> Within the next four weeks I'd like from you a detailed analysis of what's hindering our progress with affirmative action—and specific recommendations on what we can do next. Affirmative action is like other performance areas—we must set and exceed high standards.

Sam's Reflections

Sam, who has been director of affirmative action for fifteen years, came to this position after successful experiences in lower-level manufacturing management. He is a native of the Met City area, and is a respected leader in the community as well as a valued person in the organization.

He takes Bob's requests seriously. Bob is known to be results-oriented and impatient with excuses. Indeed, *Business Community*, the local business magazine, had identified him as one of the five "toughest bosses" in Met City. Sam fully intends to meet Bob's expectations.

Sam feels sure that all of the varied affirmative action actions were steps in the right direction, and he knows that senior managers believe in affirmative action; they take pride in their continuing efforts to treat everyone fairly. So the problem isn't lack of management support.

Could it be something more fundamental? At least half of the plant's employees come from rural areas surrounding Met City, where antiminority sentiments are common and where many people firmly believe that women belong at home taking care of the family. Perhaps this rural upbringing prevents many employees from being tolerant of minorities and female workers. Considering these long-standing beliefs, Sam concludes that it is time for something new. He reasons that if he has to bet his job, he should go with something other than what has been tried before and proved inadequate.

Sam's Recommendations

Sam keeps an ongoing file of materials on new affirmative action programs and evolving concepts. He starts by separating his information on new training alternatives into three categories.

1. *Refinement of traditional affirmative action approaches.* Here, the focus is on reaffirming relevant legal requirements and enhancing understanding about racism and sexism. Among the training alternatives are several racism- and sexism-sensitivity awareness programs, most of which are confrontational in nature.
2. *Valuing differences.* These programs stress the value, richness, and creativity that can flow from a diverse work force. They focus on understanding individual differences and understanding their value to business.
3. *Managing diversity.* These programs stress the importance of developing a managerial environment that "enables" all members of a diverse work force without advantaging or disadvantaging anyone.

After much consideration, Sam recommends adopting a managing diversity approach. It's a risky decision for him. Although he's attended one seminar on managing diversity, he really knows very little about it. What he does know leaves him aware that he won't be able to sell the initiative by pointing to an organization that has "done" it. In addition, managing diversity does not "fit" readily with what Met City has been about.

Still, he is personally committed to making real progress in the area of diversity, and he knows that managing diversity offers the potential for achieving significant strategic gain. Also, Sam is a veteran affirmative action manager. He knows from experience that when a window opens, you must take advantage of it quickly, because affirmative action is among the first areas to be cut back when corporations hit a rough period. He realizes that Bob has opened that window.

From what little he knows, Sam is aware that the managing diversity process starts with evaluating the corporate culture and human resources systems to uncover factors that hinder, or help. He also realizes that he doesn't have sufficient data, so he arranges for a culture audit of the Met City plant. An independent consultant is hired to conduct the audit.

Culture Audit Findings

The culture audit has two parts: it identifies the assumptions that compose the plant's culture, and then assesses whether the human resources systems, the "people systems," foster or hinder the effective management of a diverse work force.

The audit report identifies four significant cultural "roots":

1. *Fair treatment is the foundation of good management.* This assumption is the cornerstone of Compound's approach to management. Whenever a tough decision has to be made, the question of fairness is the controlling guideline.
2. *Plant engineering is the central and most highly esteemed function.* All general plant managers have been engineers who have spent time in plant engineering.
3. *The "doer" model of management is preferred.* "Doer" managers "manage" the business and people as if they are very different entities.
4. *"We are a family."* This assumption means that employees should be treated as family members. As a result, some managers have, according to the research data, behaved like dictatorial, all-knowing, and caring fathers. Others have given hiring preferences to members of employees' families. This assumption has also resulted in excellent

employee benefits, and employees have responded with extreme loyalty.

The "people systems" examination finds that:

1. *Sponsoring (advocacy) is an important determinant of promotions to senior levels.* Sponsors make the case for their candidates. They vouch for the candidates' performance and potential, and even push for them to receive promotions. Rarely, however, does a senior manager sponsor women or minorities. The researchers conclude that the sponsoring system does not work for minorities and women.
2. *Minorities and women consider performance feedback to be inadequate.* Many report not knowing where they stand or what is required to qualify for advancement.
3. *The majority of employees report dissatisfaction with the quality of developmental attention received from their supervisors.* This is a generalized condition, but minorities and women are especially critical.

Bob reviews the findings of the culture audit with Sam and asks him for recommendations on moving forward with managing diversity at Compound. He asks Sam to analyze the data and suggest which roots and systems might need changing. He also asks what else might need attention.

Sam analyzes the findings of the culture audit by addressing the following three questions:

1. What is Compound's status quo with respect to managing a diverse work force?
2. Which individual, group, and organizational factors currently hinder managing diversity at Compound Products?
3. Which individual, group, and organizational factors currently facilitate managing diversity?

The Status Quo

The Met City plant has a diverse group of employees, and top management has worked hard to foster good relationships with and among the various groups. Up until now, the plant has measured its success with affirmative action in terms of numbers: how many minorities and women are hired by and retained in the organization, and how many are represented in upper levels of management. While Sam is troubled by the continuing incidents of racism and sexism and the lack of minority and female representation in upper management levels, it is not clear that other members of the organization share his concern. Bob, the general manager, appears to be interested, but his interest reflects his concern for overall achievement. It is not based on any particular commitment to affirmative action.

Met City appears not to be experiencing organizational pain at this time. As a result, there is no urgency to resolving the "visible" diversity issues and no vision that could drive the need to take action. This means that the organization is at risk. If the plant doesn't move to manage its current challenge—retention and promotion of employees defined as "diverse"—it will begin to experience morale and productivity problems.

Hindering Factors

The culture audit suggests several forces that are likely to hinder Met City's efforts at initiating a managing diversity initiative. Key among these are elements of Met City's culture. The notion that fair treatment is the foundation of good management, for example, can discourage the perception of managing diversity as a business issue. Without that perception, it's difficult to obtain commitment.

The doer model of management is also a hindrance. This model neither recognizes the empowerment of employees as a legitimate activity nor encourages managers to seek and value diversity. The view of the company as "family" is a hindrance as well. Families exclude outsiders; boundaries are relatively impenetrable; inclusion depends on birth, marriage, or adoption. When the company is your family, you're allowed to stay simply because you're a family member—not because you perform your job well. Also, the notion of family suggests paternalism, which, in turn, discourages participatory decision making.

Met City's relative success with affirmative action can also create resistance. The employees are accustomed to this traditional method and accept it as a necessary legal and business reality.

Minorities and women in particular, however, may be alarmed at a broader definition of diversity. They may fear that implementation of managing diversity will lead to diffusion of their concerns and agendas.

The company's excellent reputation works against the adoption of managing diversity. Met City is a good example of a company that has partially defined affirmative action as good public relations. Its willingness to contribute to the right organizations and support appropriate charitable activities has earned it a reputation for being supportive of both minority communities and women. This external excellence can be misread as reflecting internal excellence or the absence of problems, leading to the misperception that "all is well."

Bob's "results" orientation may also create barriers. His emphasis on short-term results may make him impatient with initiatives that require a long-term approach. Also, his "numbers" approach may discourage him from focusing on changing mindsets—which managing diversity requires—because it is more qualitative than his usual mode of operation.

Further, the community where Met City is located can discourage the adoption of this initiative. Its norms and traditions don't support the notion of upward mobility for either minorities or women. Community members have generally been accepting of affirmative action, at least in the abstract, but they have been anxious lest it be carried "too far."

Met City's existing human resources systems will hinder managing diversity adoption and development too. The system of sponsorship does not work well for minorities and women, and performance appraisal is inadequate; minorities and women report uncertainty as to where they stand and what is required to qualify for advancement. The company's system of developing people for promotion is inadequate also. All employees suffer, but the effect falls particularly hard on minorities and women.

Bob lacks awareness of what managing diversity is about. He's familiar with affirmative action, and thinks within that framework. Educating Bob will require considerable effort.

At Met City, "diversity" is defined in narrow, traditional terms—it means minorities and women—and that will hinder the effort too. Effective implementation requires broadening the concept to include multiple dimensions. Failure to do so will seriously compromise the possibility for success.

Facilitating Factors

Offsetting these potential barriers to managing diversity are several facilitating factors, the most critical being the openness and courage of both men. Regardless of his motives, Bob's willingness to put managing diversity on his agenda bodes well for success. Sam's willingness to place his reputation and prestige on the line and boldly promote the managing diversity alternative is a significant facilitating factor as well.

Met City has already made some investment in managing diversity: Sam attended a seminar, and the culture audit was done. The more invested, the greater the pressure to make the investment pay off.

Met City's progressive affirmative action image, which can be a hindrance, can also be a positive force. The company's pride in its pacesetter status may make it more willing to pioneer managing diversity. Also, its track record with affirmative action and valuing differences suggests that the company may be willing to expand its vision when given the chance to do so.

The fact that there is substantial racial and gender diversity at Met City also helps. If the company were perceived as having a homogeneous work force, management would have more trouble accepting managing diversity as a relevant issue.

The Challenge

With this look at the hindering and facilitating factors, the challenging nature of Sam's task becomes clear. It is formidable—but not unexpected. By definition, pioneering requires that you go where others fear to tread. Significant hindrances are part of the territory.

Managing diversity calls for more than changing individual behaviors or initiating a single-focus program. It requires a change in the corporation's way of life. Such a change requires commitment and vision on the part of senior management. Sam's and Bob's continued interest and leadership skills are critical. It is not yet completely clear whether Sam is prepared to accept the responsibilities of a change agent.

The Plan

Given the realities of the situation, Sam's decision to advance with managing diversity means that he must incorporate elements from all three approaches: affirmative action, valuing differences, and managing diversity. He develops a three-pronged plan.

1. Affirmative Action Recommendations

▪ *Continue Met City's outstanding affirmative action program.* Although the hope is that managing diversity will eventually make affirmative action unnecessary, this is not likely to happen within the next fifteen years.

▪ *Given the continuing incidents of racial and sexual discrimination, expand affirmative action remedial education.* Met City seems to have done a good job of initially informing people of what affirmative action laws and regulations require, but continuing refresher courses are needed.

▪ *Offer "Requirements for Success at Met City" courses to* all employees. Here the goal is to help employees—white males as well as blacks, women, Hispanics, and Asian Americans—understand what they have to do to achieve upward mobility. They can then make an informed decision as to whether to conform.

At first glance, this third recommendation seems to conflict with the concept of managing diversity. Yet the reality is that for the foreseeable future, individuals will continue to bear the brunt of the adaptation process. Assimilation will be the dominant mode until managing diversity matures.

The goal of the recommendation is to enhance creation of a diverse cadre of women and minority managers at the higher levels, yet—in the spirit of managing diversity—the courses are available to *all* employee groups. This minimizes the likelihood that white males or others will complain about perceived unfair advantages.

2. Valuing Differences Recommendations

▪ *Continue or reinstitute sensitivity or awareness training for individuals.* This would reaffirm previous attempts to foster an appreciation and understanding of the differences that people bring to the workplace. Its intent is to foster enhanced interpersonal relations among members of diverse groups.

Similar programs have been done in the past—with temporary effects. In addition, valuing differences initiatives are more likely to be effective when organizations are experiencing overt conflicts that clearly call for resolution. The more limited and subtle problems that continue to crop up at Met City are more difficult to address.

3. Managing Diversity Recommendations

▪ *Imbue the organization with an understanding of how diversity relates to Met City's vision.* Doing this requires that managers "buy in" to a diversity vision, relate it to the overall vision of the plant, and communicate their support and vision to their employees so that everyone is pursuing the same vision.

▪ *Help managers and employees clarify their motivation for a managing diversity initiative by identifying it as the business issue it is.* This becomes particularly important given the current lack of pain and the limited vision with respect to managing diversity. The goal is to develop a clear, convincing case that managing diversity is connected to the continued viability of the Met City facility.

▪ *Educate managers—senior, middle, and entry level—about the nature of managing diversity and how it differs from valuing differences and affirmative action.* This involves significant changes in mindset: the difference between doer and empowering managers, the breadth of diversity, and the fact that managing diversity is primarily for the manager's benefit and not that of minorities and women. To help managers understand managing diversity fully, education will continue throughout the change process.

▪ *Educate the rank and file on managing diversity and the ways it differs from valuing differences and affirmative action.* Several cost-effective and efficient techniques can be used, ranging from articles to speeches to brief video presentations followed by discussion.

• *Change Met City's culture.* Yes, this is easier said than done! Yet it must be accomplished, because at least three of the four roots identified in the culture audit have a substantial potential to hinder managing diversity. Several options or combinations of options can be useful:

— Educate senior managers about the process of changing, maintaining, and managing corporate culture. It is important that these managers be comfortable with the concept of culture and also knowledgeable about levers available for changing it.

— Have senior managers identify the root changes they want to make. It's important that they be specific about what these changes should entail and how extensive they should be.

— Once the desired changes have been identified, develop a plan for implementing and institutionalizing them.

Here, an example may help. Consider this cultural root: "The doer model of management is preferred." Suppose Met City's senior managers decide to retain this root but supplement it with the empowerment model. The task here is not to yank out the doer manager root but to allow it to intertwine with an empowerment root.

To make this root change, managers will take every chance they get to articulate the new doer/empowerment root. They may also work this notion into all the company's human resources systems. For example, one factor in deciding promotions will now be the potential to use the doer and empowerment models jointly.

• *Change Met City's "people" systems.* Since the culture audit showed that the sponsoring, performance appraisal, and developmental processes all work against managing diversity, all three are prospects for systemic change. Involve these steps:

— Examine each system in detail and identify patterns that work against the effective management of diversity. Also, ferret out what is generating these patterns.

— Identify what must be done to eliminate the undesirable patterns and convert the system to a facilitating factor.
— Develop a plan for implementing the desired changes.

For example, one of the major findings of the culture audit was that the informal sponsoring process does not work for women and minorities. If sponsoring is to continue, there must be a monitoring process that holds sponsors accountable. Individual sponsors who repeatedly sponsor only people like themselves represent a managing diversity challenge. Managing diversity requires that managers develop a capability for naturally sponsoring a group of diverse individuals that reflects the diversity of the total work force. At a minimum this requires that they understand the dynamics of sponsoring.

Such understanding would include why people come to sponsor certain individuals and how others are screened out. It would also require that understanding be followed by action. It may be, for example, that a sponsor has a pattern of sponsoring people with whom he comes in daily contact. If all the people he interacts with are like himself, corrective action may be relatively simple: his sphere of contact can be expanded to give him an opportunity to interact with those who reflect the total work force. A cautionary note: We are not suggesting quotas. We are talking about eliminating a system of barriers that for whatever reason causes the sponsorship process not to work effectively for all people.

What could we expect to happen if the recommendations were followed? Let's look ahead five years, one year at a time. (All actions and outcomes are summarized in Exhibit 5-1.)

YEAR ONE

Action 1. Once Bob accepted his recommendations, Sam was faced with a decision. Considering the magnitude of the changes needed, did he *really* want to take on the role of change agent? He sat down and listed a series of questions:

Where am I on this issue of managing diversity?
What does it mean to me?
Why is it important?

Exhibit 5-1. Managing diversity at Compound Products, Inc.

Year	Action Steps	Outcomes
1	Self-analysis	Personal clarity and conviction on part of Sam
	Recruitment of allies	
	Education of boss	Buy-in from boss and allies
	Proposal of combined initiative	
	Establishment of task force	
	Presentation of a planning session for task force	
	Presentation of planning session for Bob's direct reports	Task force and Bob's cabinet are positioned to play leadership role
2	Design and presentation of affirmative action programs to rank and file	Enhanced sensitivity to requirements of affirmative action
	Design and presentation of half of planned valuing diversity sessions	Enhanced acceptance and tolerance of differences
	Planning sessions for Bob's direct reports and their managers	Greater understanding in managerial ranks of affirmative action, valuing differences, and managing diversity
	Presentation of team-building session for task force	Better sense of purpose and organization among task force members
3	Completion of valuing differences programs	Enhanced acceptance and tolerance of differences
	Initiation of managing diversity training for employees	Enhanced rank and file understanding of managing diversity
	Presentation of planning session for Bob and his direct reports	Greater commitment on the part of Bob and direct reports
	Establishment of joint committee	
4	Completion of joint committee's report	Enhanced sense that company is serious about managing diversity
	Integration of managing diversity into existing training programs	Greater awareness of managerial, cultural, and system changes that will be required
		Institutionalization of managing diversity educational efforts
5	Presentation of series of management training sessions	Greater readiness to move forward with managerial, cultural, and system changes.

What am I willing or unwilling to do to move managing diversity forward?

Am I willing to be a lead change agent? If not, how do I recruit someone who is?

Do I have sufficient power to do what I want to do or, alternately, do I have the support of individuals with sufficient power? Most important, where is Bob on this matter? Can I trust him to do what is necessary to move this forward?

Over the next three months, he pondered the questions, talking with his wife and close colleagues. He also attended a personal development seminar to learn more about his personal style and preferences.

After this period of analysis, he decided that he *would* assume the change agent role but that he would plan and execute his efforts with care. He was willing to take the risk, but he knew he would need help. So he decided to look for allies and to be certain that Bob was in his corner before proceeding further.

Action 2. Sam spent the next two months seeking out allies. He talked one-on-one to several minority and women managers to identify those who might be willing to serve on a diversity task force. Their interest in the task force encouraged him to expand his efforts further.

Next, he met with four line managers who had seemed particularly interested in the culture audit. They, too, were willing to serve on the task force. Then Sam moved horizontally, and got commitments to serve on the task force from representatives of all Met City's major functions.

Action 3. During this time, Sam was active on another front as well. His goal was to educate Bob. He decided, first, to take advantage of the greater impact that information from an outside source can have. He asked the consultant to conduct an initial briefing with Bob. Following this, he scheduled several conversations between Bob and himself over the course of a month. At the end of this time, Bob was ready to consider and evaluate more in-depth information. The consultant returned for a series of conversations.

Action 4. Finally, Bob seemed ready to commit himself, but Sam was uneasy. Bob's support was too important to take any chances. He sensed that Bob was uncomfortable with the conceptual, theoretical orientation that is integral to managing diversity. He knew, also, that Bob valued action.

That's why, in part, Sam had decided to propose the three-part plan with affirmative action and valuing differences.

He hoped it would ensure Bob's commitment to managing diversity while meeting his need for visible results. In particular, alleviating the problem of racist and sexist incidents at the plant through valuing differences training would help Bob tolerate the longer, more complex efforts needed to launch managing diversity. Sam was right. The combined plan appealed to Bob's desire for "hands on" action and sealed his commitment to the managing diversity initiative.

Action 5. Seven months into the first year, Sam called the first meeting of the task force. During the next few months, the task force met several times to organize, determine their purpose and function, and add more members.

Action 6. Sam determined that the task force was ready for a planning session, and called the consultant back again.

In the planning session, the consultant helped task force members to do the following:
- Explore differences among affirmative action, valuing differences, and managing diversity.
- Examine managing diversity in the context of Met City's vision and strategy.
- Determine whether managing diversity is a business issue for Met City.
- Identify, at least in an armchair way, basic components of Met City's culture.
- Assess whether Met City's culture supports managing diversity.
- Review and digest details of the culture audit.
- Determine "next steps" for further implementing managing diversity.

A major outcome here was the conclusion that managing diversity was a business issue for Met City.

Action 7. During this same period, Sam held a similar planning session with Bob and Bob's direct reports.

Recommendations

Several recommendations were made as a result of this first year's efforts:

- Affirmative action and valuing differences sessions should be designed and implemented vigorously over the next twelve months.
- Each of Bob's direct reports and the managers reporting to them should go through planning sessions so as to educate senior management and push the mindset changes down through the organization. In all, there would be as many sessions as the number of Bob's reports.

- Planning should begin for educating the general employee population in the managing diversity initiative.

Outcomes

Sam's first year of effort toward managing diversity resulted in several positive outcomes.

- Sam was clear about what he wanted to do and at peace with his role as a change agent.
- He had Bob firmly on board, and he had a group of allies in place in the form of the task force.
- He had held several planning sessions for task force members, and for Bob and his direct reports.
- As a result, those people who would take the lead in implementing managing diversity were clear about managing diversity's business rationale and the specific mandates as to their "next step" priorities.

YEAR TWO

Action 1. During year two, the affirmative action training programs were designed and presented to both managers and rank and file members. These programs covered the legal ramifications of discrimination and equal opportunity, with particular attention given to practical tips for staying within legal constraints.

Design for the valuing differences programs was completed and presentation of these programs was started. In these programs, participants explored how various employee groups differed, surfaced their own predispositions toward differences, and developed strategies for enhancing their ability to work effectively with people who were different.

Midway through the planned valuing differences sessions, however, task force members became concerned about a training overload. They recommended that the second half of the valuing differences programs and all of the programs designed to introduce managing diversity to the employees be postponed until year three. These recommendations were accepted and training efforts put temporarily on hold.

Action 2. Planning sessions were conducted for Bob's direct reports and their managers.

Action 3. Task force members, aware of some fragmentation and confusion, asked for and were given a team-building session. Its purpose: to reaffirm the task force's objectives and help members plan for year three.

Recommendations

Recommendations coming out of the session included the following:

- Complete the valuing differences training in year three.
- Conduct employee training regarding managing diversity in year three.
- Hold another planning session for Bob and his direct reports to get their suggestions on next steps for years three and four.

Outcomes

Year two efforts achieved several important results:

- Managers and employees were more sensitive to the requirements of affirmative action.
- Those managers and employees who attended valuing differences sessions were more sensitive to understanding, accepting, and appreciating the differences that people bring to the workplace.
- Managers were more accepting of the three approaches to managing diversity. This acceptance led to a greater readiness to talk about what needed to be done to move forward with managing diversity at Met City as a whole and in the respective departments.
- Task force members had a better sense of purpose and organization among themselves. The team-building process helped them to feel more like a team, have greater commitment to the change agent role, and have better understanding of its implications.

YEAR THREE

Actions 1, 2. During year three, Met City completed its valuing differences programs and began employee training on managing diversity.

Action 3. Sam conducted another planning session with Bob and his direct reports. This session resulted in a recognition, based on their understanding of managing diversity, that they needed to examine and modify the role and definition of management at Met City. They also expressed their readiness to address culture and systems changes.

Action 4. Sam, sensing that the time was right, encouraged the establishment of a joint committee—some representatives of the task force, some of the senior managers. After a few weeks of jostling for position, negotiating, and cajoling, the committee met. Overall, the joint committee was charged with identifying the changes in Met City's culture, the role of its managers, and the company's "people" systems that were needed for effective implementation of managing diversity to take place. During year three, however, the committee members contented themselves with assessing and becoming more comfortable with the issues.

Outcomes

▪ People who had completed the valuing differences program in year three were more aware of what is required to be an effective member of a diverse work force.

▪ Rank and file members had a mindset congruent with that of their managers. They understood that there are three approaches, were aware of management's efforts to implement managing diversity, and had begun to think about what they needed to do to start moving ahead with the initiative.

▪ Bob and his direct reports were increasingly committed to the managing diversity initiative. They had a better understanding of what is needed for success and were eager to move forward. The creation of the joint committee during the third quarter represented a major implementation step.

YEAR FOUR

Action 1. Year four was essentially a time of consolidation. Members of the joint committee met regularly, and in the fourth quarter, they presented a report. A key feature of this report was a detailed blueprint as to how the role of the manager and the organization's culture should change. The committee's report highlighted the need to adopt the empowerment model of management and to have managers play both a leadership role and a management role. The report assumed the leadership was willing to bring about needed cultural (root) changes.

Among the highlights of the blueprint developed by the joint committee were several recommendations:

—Senior management should redefine the plant's operating definition of management to include greater reliance on the empowerment model.

—The plant's root configuration should be changed to downplay "family." While realizing that further study would be required before definitive details could be cast in concrete, the committee noted strong member sentiment for "We should behave as a team" as the governing root.

—The plant's root configuration should be changed to reflect the strategic need to tap the full potential of *all* employees. In particular, members believed that this new root should replace the emphasis on fairness as the foundation of good management.

—The plant's people systems should be examined and changed as necessary to support managing diversity. Special attention was to be given to performance appraisal and sponsoring.

Although committee members had strong views and recognized that they were calling for major change, they desired to convey their positions in a manner that would not preclude involvement by the plant population. They realized fully that much discussion and planning would be required to make their recommendations reality. As a next step, the committee felt that the education and buy-in of the plant managers should be pursued.

Action 2. Paralleling this major committee project was an effort to integrate managing diversity education into all ongoing training activities. This effort was propelled and monitored by the original diversity task force, which also monitored training programs started in earlier years. Their integration initiatives resulted in the following:

—Development programs for senior management examined how leadership in support of managing diversity could be provided.

—Middle-management sessions explored the perspective of the white male and how he could facilitate managing diversity.

—In each program, modules dealing with integrating the doer and empowerment models were introduced.

—Modules for the new manager presented projections of work force demographics and allowed opportunity for the discussion of implications.

Outcomes

▪ Year four was a watershed period as people began to recognize how much time and energy the plant as a whole and its managers and task force members had put forth toward the managing diversity effort. The general perception developed that "management is serious here." This perception led, in turn, to the increased commitment of individuals as they sensed the potential for real and lasting change.

▪ Joint committee members made a qualitative shift when they moved from a conceptual understanding of managing diversity to a determination to identify and initiate the changes needed for its implementation. Committee members now wanted to know, "How do we get on with empowerment management? How do we get on with root change? How do we get on with changing systems?" The answers began to get clearer in year four.

▪ The integration of managing diversity into Met City's ongoing programs represented an institutionalization of managing diversity as an accepted way of addressing diversity. Without such institutionalization, the possibility of lasting change would be minimal.

Results have appeared, but they are not *too* tangible, and yet, they are major:

- Widespread understanding and buy-in have been achieved with respect to affirmative action, valuing differences, and managing diversity.
- Awareness *and* buy-in regarding the kinds of system and cultural changes that will be required.
- Readiness to proceed with cultural and systems changes is evident.
- Initial steps have been taken to institutionalize managing diversity.

As an indication of the magnitude of these accomplishments, I note that I am unaware of *any* corporation that has attained this level of implementation.

YEAR FIVE

Action 1. Equipped with the joint committee recommendations, Sam and the diversity task force planned and oversaw the presentation of a series of training sessions for senior management, to help them understand:
—What changes were desired in the managerial process.
—What the empowerment model of management is and how it can complement/supplement the doer model.
—The difference between the leadership and management roles and the need for managers to play both roles.
—What is involved in fostering culture change and the role of the manager in doing so.
Senior managers attending the workshop were expected to develop a blueprint detailing how they could foster culture change in Met City in general and in their organization in particular by the end of the year.

Their work was, of course, done within the context of the joint committee's blueprint for the kinds of changes that would be required. The committee's understanding was, in turn, based on the findings of the culture audit.

Action 2. At the request of Bob and his direct reports, Sam recruited and hired a work/family coordinator. This individual was charged with identifying critical work/family issues and preparing a plan for addressing them.

Action 3. Concerned that they not fall into the trap of defining diversity narrowly, Bob directed Sam to appoint a functional diversity subcommittee. Its principal objective was to ensure that changes underway or planned fostered effective management of functional diversity.

Outcomes

■ All senior managers participated in the management training workshops, which indicates a readiness to move forward with change in the culture and systems.

As the company moves into year six, the issue now becomes, will they be able to move forward with the mechanism of culture change, and also put in place supporting systems to ensure that they carry out what has been learned in year five? Individually, senior managers approached cultural change differently. For example, consider manager A and manager B.

Manager A determined that buy-in would be difficult for many of his senior subordinates, so he proposed three initial steps to facilitate "unfreezing":

1. Raise the possibility of culture change in continual one-on-one dialogues with his direct reports.
2. Talk up the possibility of culture change in his presentations to various employee groups.
3. Circulate information on changing demographics and other environmental realities fostering the need for culture change.

Then, when his organizational unit is ready to consider culture change, he plans to move to other actions:

4. Convene a one-day session to begin exploring the kinds of culture changes that should be made. (Manager A is prepared to go back to the joint committee with any sugges-

tions that go beyond their blueprint. He felt that a sense of ownership would greatly facilitate the buy-in of his senior people, so he is willing to risk that their developing recommendations would not be totally congruent with the joint committee's work.)

5. Continue the informal dialogue in an attempt to secure allies for moving in the direction of the desired change.
6. Convene another one-day session with direct reports to finalize thinking about culture change and to begin exploring implementation vehicles.

Manager A estimated that all these steps would require eight to twelve months.

Manager B believed that employees in her unit were already informally calling for the cultural changes reflected in the joint committee's blueprint. As a result she planned to move much more quickly to focus on implementation, through the following measures:

- Convene two one-day sessions of her direct reports to refine their thinking on the desired changes and to begin developing implementation approaches.
- Encourage direct reports to explore through task forces (a) implications of culture changes for modifying people systems (here she believes that her unit could take the lead in what eventually would be a plantwide dialogue), (b) implications for changing their orientation of new employees, and (c) implications for changing the unit's priorities.

Chapter 6

Research: First Steps Toward Managing Diversity — Culberson Industries

The Defense Application Laboratory (DAL) of Culberson Industries' defense products division has the responsibility for developing new defense products. The technology involved is often "top secret." Once the government declassifies a technology, DAL researches possible consumer applications. The defense products division then licenses the most viable possibilities to its sister Culberson divisions, all of which manufacture and market a wide range of consumer products. Indeed, historically over 30 percent of the division's net profits have come from this source.

In the 1960s and 1970s, DAL earned a reputation as being the affirmative action front-runner within the division and the company. Through aggressive recruitment and hiring, the laboratory brought on board significant numbers of women and minority professionals, despite the relatively small size of the national pools from which it recruited. The laboratory's location in a West Coast academic community facilitated recruitment efforts.

Once these individuals were on board, DAL pioneered a variety of interventions within Culberson: sensitivity training for white male managers, corporate survival training for minorities

Note: This chapter presents an actual case study of a Fortune 500 company. The company's name and description have been disguised; the data have not.

and women, laboratory-wide affirmative action training, and mentoring programs for minorities and women. Because of these efforts DAL's management took pride in their affirmative action accomplishments.

Approximately four years ago, complaints from blacks began filtering up to senior management. These concerns surprised the managers, for they thought all was well. For a year or so, they did not consider the grievances to be credible. But they continued and grew in number and visibility.

Initially, management gave consideration to reinstituting some of the initiatives of the 1960s and 1970s, but backed away from this option because several managers still had difficulty giving much weight to the expressions of concerns. Four basic questions were raised:

1. How widespread were the complaints?
2. What did the black employees want?
3. What factors were causing the problems?
4. What were the possible solutions?

These questions and the related uncertainty led management to commission a research project on black professionals. The purpose of the research was to provide a framework for designing and launching interventions to (1) consolidate DAL's affirmative action gains and (2) to set the stage for further progress through the effective management of employee diversity. Specifically management wanted the research to identify and examine the dynamics of the laboratory's people systems (recruitment, selection, training, development, and promotions) as they were experienced by black employees. In sum, management hoped that the research would help them get a handle on "black issues."

One other consideration should be mentioned: DAL's management elected to focus on successful blacks, primarily because the management wanted to minimize excessive negativism and to learn about what had worked in fostering the development and productivity of the black employees.

Two years ago, DAL did some research on the factors that contributed to the success of the company's black managers. From this research came an unusual recommendation: Perhaps

DAL needed a better way of developing managerial talent—*all* managers, not just black managers.

So a second research project was begun, one that examined the "people development" experiences of all managers—Hispanics, blacks, white women, Asian/Pacific Islander men and women, and white males. The goal was to determine what patterns of factors and experiences enabled employees to grow. Of special interest were boss-subordinate relationships, mentoring relationships, opportunities for formal training, and work assignment patterns.

The decision to do the second project represented a major transitional step toward managing diversity. Particularly noteworthy was the inclusion of white males at a time when organizations that addressed diversity issues often attempted to take a "color blind" approach, and even those that did acknowledge diversity's breadth still excluded white males. It is not overly dramatic to call DAL a true pioneer.

The research report that came out of the study offers a rich framework for understanding the experiences of the different employee groups and for moving ahead with creating an environment in which the potential of all managers could be tapped.

The Interviews

The basic research tool was the one-on-one interview, using a thirteen-question format. Five groups of managers—twenty-seven blacks, nineteen Hispanics, nineteen white women, twenty-one Asians/Pacific Islanders, and twenty-three white males—were included in the study. Their length of service with the company spanned three to twenty-three years; their organizational levels ranged from group leader (experienced technologists) to laboratory director. All participants were viewed as having successful careers with DAL and were rated at least average.

Interview questions (see Appendix 6A) were concerned with uncovering participants' perceptions in five general areas:

1. The reasons they had selected and remained with DAL
2. What had determined their success
3. The quality of their work assignments and of the supervision they had received

4. Barriers that hampered further upward mobility
5. The laboratory's overall success in managing diversity

Highlights of the Findings

The full results of these interviews are reported in tabular form in
Appendix 6B; highlights are summarized here.

Selection and Retention. Overall, participants reported that
they felt good about their employment and that the factors that
had attracted them to DAL were the ones that encouraged them
to stay. Generally speaking, the diverse groups responded similarly to this group of questions, but the emphasis varied from
group to group.

White men, white women, and Hispanics reported being attracted primarily by the nature of the work; blacks and Asians/
Pacific Islanders were more impressed by the combination of people encountered during the interview process and the security
and stability of the company. The nature of the work was also
cited by white males as the most important reason for *remaining*
with DAL. Other groups also thought this was important, but
they differed in the emphasis they gave it.

When asked why they might contemplate leaving, all
groups—but minorities more than others—cited problem supervisors and concerns about reward and recognition. However,
most respondents felt that their expectations had been met at
DAL. White men and white women were the most satisfied, although white women indicated concern about the apparent "ceil-
ings" blocking the director and vice-president levels. Blacks, Hispanics, and Asians/Pacific Islanders qualified their positive
sentiments by reporting concern about advancement, development, management, and the nature of the work. The individuals
most dissatisfied among minority groups were those who had
been with the company for over fifteen years.

Determinants of Success. When asked to identify the key to
their success, most participants named the chance to participate
in a decision-making role in important work (that is, having the

"right assignment"). For white men and white women, the chance to work under a helpful manager was also very important. Many, in fact, saw key work assignments under a helpful manager as representing a critical turning point in their careers.

Blacks, however, were more likely to cite a collection of meaningful work experiences under supportive managers than a key event or person. And they believed that technical accomplishment was almost as important as the "right assignment"; for Asians, it was the most important of all. As a group, Hispanics saw the ability to work with people as being almost as important as the right assignment and helpful managers.

Mentoring. All groups—but to varying degrees—had mentors, and all believed that it was important to success, particularly in their early years. Their mentors performed several roles—counselors, sponsors, protectors, rescuers, sources of insight on DAL—in addition to giving feedback on performance.

Quality of Supervision. Participants from each group reported experiencing an uneven quality of supervision; they readily acknowledged receiving some quality supervision, but they also indicated that they had had some very poor managers. Supervisory problems were also cited as one of two key reasons for considering leaving the company at some point. This is from a Hispanic participant:

> Overall, the quality has been excellent. I have always felt lucky. . . . Others that I have known have not been as lucky. I have seen people burn two or three years of their careers because of poor supervision.

Barriers to Advancement. Responses to this group of questions indicated that white men experienced relatively few barriers to advancement. Each of the other groups saw significant barriers and were specific in their comments. All minorities and women believed that their main barrier was being pigeonholed because of their race, education, or style. They perceived management as uninformed about managing diversity and overcommitted to assimilation.

White women cited "being female" as their major barrier. They felt that management was uncomfortable with women, and that they received inadequate feedback and were excluded from the informal network. Hispanics perceived a stereotyping and a bias against their culture. One Hispanic manager described the situation this way:

> Stereotypical assumptions are a barrier; for example, I am viewed as having a hot temper and being prone to violence because of my background. One manager actually told me that I was prone to violence because of my background. When these things happen, I stop the meeting and put it on the table. This is stressful, but effective. I have not had to do this too many times lately. I should not have to go through this.

Asians/Pacific Islanders cited twin barriers: "being pigeonholed as technologists (technical coolies)" and "being discriminated against" because of their cultural style. For example:

> It is a consensus among the Asians that they are hired because they are technically strong, and that they are tagged as technical people, not as people who can be trained as managers. You have to treat people equally. We are not asking for an advantage, but are asking for opportunity.

Blacks saw "racism" as their principal challenge. They were particularly concerned about the informality and ambiguity that characterized upward movement to the higher levels. As one black manager said:

> One barrier to me has been a lack of a clear developmental plan or strategy that could be shared by the supervisors. There is an assumption that once you have been with a company for ten years, you no longer need support on career planning. You become responsible for your career. Unless you have a mentor high in the orga-

nization, people at the section-head level are left pretty much to chart their own destiny.

An important barrier from groups who came from outside the United States (Asians and Hispanics) was difficulty in communication.

The Company and the Future. DAL wanted to know how participants perceived the laboratory's ability to create an environment that enables all employees and also what were their thoughts on how greater progress might be realized. Some felt that managers needed to better understand and value the groups represented within the organization. This is from a white woman manager:

> There needs to be an understanding that women are fundamentally different from men and why that is good. And, an understanding that women do not have to act like men to be effective. We have to get everyone in the organization to realize that there are inherently female advantages that can be utilized.

A black manager says:

> Risks taken on the part of top management and senior management regarding developmental opportunities for blacks is an issue—especially with respect to individuals who have been here for a while. These persons must be treated as others with whom risks are taken. Philosophy of "safe blacks" has to go.

Some respondents reported that they wanted their managers to help them assimilate to desired DAL behavior. From one Asian interviewee:

> There is a difference in the awareness of overseas and American-born Asians or Orientals. There is a need to grow out of cultural differences that Orientals have

around humbleness and passiveness. Individuals should work around language differences and verbal differences. American-born Asians do not have these problems. There should be open career discussions. People should be helped (by their managers) with these differences. Individuals wish to move beyond these differences and the corporation should be willing to help them.

White women managers noted that although the company had made some allowances for major family responsibilities, more needed to be done. They were concerned about how junior white women managers would feel. A senior white woman manager had this to say:

We need to figure how we are going to deal with the pain young white women will have to encounter when they have to make choices. . . . At some point, the personal pain level will leap tremendously. The laboratory has only started to make accommodations that will be necessary for working mothers. Being a working mother will constitute the first personal pain for many of these young women, and I'm not just talking about the need for day care systems. They raise the issue of management of time. If we do not deal with the issue, there is a danger that we will lose a high percentage of these individuals—especially if we assume that all employees have wives at home to take care of their kids.

White male managers, in particular, noted a need to enhance managers' ability to manage people *in general*.

We need to develop a school on leadership and management, and to look at management as a technology. There needs to be a clear mission, strategy, and set of tools around managing people. Presently, there is no integration of approaches.

What We Can Learn From the Findings

Complexity of Diversity

One of the most important understandings that came out of this study was the *complexity* of diversity—that there was a great range of differences both *among* and *within* the various groups.

For example, although the different groups were alike in seeking more opportunities, they focused on different hierarchical positions. White women and blacks were aiming at director and vice-president slots; Hispanics and Asian Americans sought more movement in general.

Also, differences within groups abounded. This might appear to be obvious, but it was not uncommon, for example, to hear individuals talk as if all blacks were relatively new employees with strong desires to be promoted. In reality, the interviewed black managers differed significantly in their goals, linked mainly to length of time with the laboratory. Black managers who had been with DAL for three to nine years were, in fact, upwardly mobile and anticipating considerable advancement opportunity. Black managers who had been with the laboratory for ten to fifteen years were more cautious about the future and concerned that they might have plateaued. Many black managers who had been with the laboratory for sixteen to twenty-two years felt that they *had* plateaued.

There were differences in other groups as well. Senior and junior white women managers, for example, experienced different types of challenges. And both Asian and Hispanic respondents varied greatly in their degree of assimilation to American culture. Some considered themselves members of America's mainstream and in need of no special assistance or preferential treatment. Others, more comfortable with their ethnic culture than with their adopted one, wanted help in understanding and adapting to DAL's culture.

The breadth of the differences within the groups resulted in diminished cohesiveness within the Hispanic and Asian/Pacific Islander groups and made it difficult for them to formulate and achieve joint goals. To make matters worse, Hispanics and Asians/ Pacific Islanders were reluctant to participate in affirmative action because of the stigma associated with it.

As a result, members of these groups viewed themselves as the "forgotten minorities." They felt that their needs had not been addressed. One respondent said, "The Asian/Pacific Islander issue is in its infancy." A Hispanic respondent made a similar comment:

> Until this research effort, I did not feel that the laboratory had addressed at all the needs of minorities other than blacks. My career has been fought on technical and personal grounds, and I think that is right. There has been no commitment to Hispanics like that that has been given to blacks and women. I don't think the effort has been extended to the Hispanic manager.

The Difficulty of Assimilation

Another key understanding to flow from the research was the degree of difficulty with which some minority respondents understood and adapted to DAL's culture and the high price paid by many who had successfully done so.

The assimilation/adaptation approach to employee diversity works best when employees are not very diverse. It is less effective when cultural differences are great. Hispanic and Asian/Pacific Islander respondents reported major differences between their home cultures and that of DAL.

Here are statements from two Hispanic managers:

> There are several reasons why Hispanics might have difficulty in learning the system. Typically, these individuals do not come from the center of the universe. For example, Puerto Rico is not exactly the center. American kids, on the other hand, think they are the center and that they can make things happen. Also, the typical Hispanic attitude is not congruent with the system. For example, the system responds to my thinking that it is

up to me to do it. The Hispanic culture suggests that it is up to us to do it.

*   *   *

Latin Americans tend to be involving people. This means that they involve other people in deciding what needs to be done. In this culture, when you act in that manner it is perceived as not taking charge. You are perceived as taking charge only if you are pushing. The Latino culture says that you are in charge only if you involve other people who have an interest in the issue. Pulling other people in and telling them more is a plus. I am viewed, unfortunately, as not pushing enough.

Asian/Pacific Islander respondents found assimilation even more difficult as they struggled with a "classism" that defined people with impressive technical skills as lacking managerial potential. Because many Asians/Pacific Islanders were recruited as technologists, they particularly were affected by this classism.

The biggest barrier has been perceived notions about me. I am seen as a strong technologist and scientist, but it doesn't go any further. The fact that I am an Asian/ Pacific Islander . . . viewed as a strong scientist is a barrier. The lack of mentors has also been a barrier. I have supporters, but no mentors.

You must be a good salesperson. You must promote your ideas and projects. Asians are technology inclined. There is no outlet for the technologist. There is no outlet for Asians. We are set back. We are put in a box, and we cannot get out. The laboratory must develop a way to appreciate technology and the technologist. Eventually we Asians lose. Asians are in the technology hole.

For the most part, Hispanic and Asian/Pacific Islander respondents reported a willingness to adapt. Yet they perceived their personal cultural roots as assets with potential benefit for the laboratory. Many found it painful to abandon key aspects of their upbringing.

This perception of the difficulty of assimilation was validated by some respondents who had made the change. Both white women and Hispanics, for example, reported that they had assimilated into the laboratory's system but that the price had been high. A white woman manager says:

> The women who have been promoted to associate director and higher share a common style. They are extremely aggressive and appear to subordinate their personal lives for the laboratory. Many are not married. In contrast, men associate directors and up have all kinds of styles—from aggressive to quietly competent.

This is from a Hispanic manager:

> I feel amputated—like I've lost an arm. I feel angry. I have lost some of my good qualities in trying to conform. . . . My barrier primarily has been being different personality-wise rather than nationality-wise. The differences between a person who, like myself, is intuitive by nature, not very organized, and very emotional, as compared to the DAL model that stressed logic, rationality, organization, stability, and being data based. . . . I do not blame the laboratory for my having compromised. They did not tell me that I had to chop my arm off. I could have changed the hole, but I chose to chop on myself. The dominant factor here was my overwhelming desire to get ahead, even if I had to compromise. It was like becoming the teacher's pet. Whatever the teacher wanted, the teacher got.

The Limitations of Mentoring

DAL relies on an informal approach to "people development," centered around mentoring. It has worked especially well for white men, relatively well for white women, less well for minorities. Asians/Pacific Islanders, Hispanics, and blacks reported less satisfaction both with DAL in general and with the informal mentoring system in particular than did their white counterparts.

A key purpose of mentoring is, of course, to facilitate individual adaptation to the laboratory's requirements for success. Mentoring can be a very powerful development and assimilation tool for individuals who are willing and able to adapt, but it is of limited value where adaptation is undesirable or impossible.

An example: White women reported extensive mentoring experiences, and also reported that a "ceiling" kept them from promotion to top spots. The assimilation required to move into director and vice-president slots was beyond the capability of the women involved. In other words, no amount of mentoring or adaptation will result in women becoming men.

The conclusion to be drawn here is not that mentoring never works. It does, and more and better mentoring opportunities must be extended to minority groups. But if companies are to tap the full potential of their women and minorities, they must be prepared to share in the adaptation process. The concept of managing diversity is built on the assumption that adaptation is mutual; both the individual *and* the organization must make changes.

The Need for Improved Management Techniques Across the Board

DAL managers are essentially "doers." In fact, this is common in technical organizations. The manager who thinks that helping other people develop their own skills is what the manager's job is all about is rare.

> We need to learn management skills. We hire technical people who have mostly worked in a lab in an almost monastic setting. They usually do not have management skills. They need to learn how to motivate people.

> There is a tremendous preoccupation in getting the job done. This is true for managers. They get so caught up that they fail to see the importance of people. I don't think anybody believes they will get by on people development alone. Everybody realizes that this is not the

case. A large number of people do not believe that we have a people commitment to the extent that we put it in words. Although people are considered to be important, everybody will tell you that the business side is more important.

Providing opportunities for people to progress through promotions is not the same as "developing people." Minorities and women have been promoted at DAL, but this may have more to do with the substantial growth experienced in the 1960s and 1970s, which resulted in an expansion of middle management ranks, than it does with a commitment to people development and good management skills.

Management Responses

DAL managers were very receptive to the most generalized finding of the research: People within the division felt good about their jobs and the nature of their work. There was no evidence that respondents were a depressed or demoralized group of people. The data made it clear, however, that unless DAL improved its ability to develop people, it would lose some of the potential of a growing portion of its work force, minorities and women. This is the business necessity for broadening the approach to diversity. In the midst of competitive realities, the laboratory must make sure it fully uses all its human resources. It cannot afford to do less.

Acknowledgment of this reality led DAL managers to generate the following recommendations:

1. Leaders and managers must be enrolled in the process of implementing managing diversity. Because this concept is "on the cutting edge" and pioneering in nature, management's enrollment, ownership, and creativity will be critical to any successful implementation.

2. A diversity planning workshop should be made available to DAL managers, with the goal of enlisting their creativity and ideas and creating implementation plans for various organiza-

tional units within the laboratory. Workshop activities would be designed to:

- Digest the research data.
- Allow exploration of the managing diversity approach within the context of the laboratory's business realities.
- Determine the requirements of leadership and management needed to successfully implement the managing diversity approach.
- Design an implementation strategy.

3. Mentoring and sponsoring are crucial parts of the people development process, and should be made more effective. At the same time, managers must remember that the potential of such methods is limited for people who are "different."

4. The laboratory should develop a program designed to enhance its managers' ability to manage all people. Ideally, such a program should focus on the concepts, as well as the skills, of management and leadership. Participants should leave with a framework for further developing their managerial capability. In addition, the reality of employee diversity should be woven throughout the program.

5. Existing management training programs should be amended to include significant blocks of time on managing diversity.

6. DAL should establish, design, and conduct an annual conference on multicultural diversity, giving each department an opportunity to (a) present findings and results of efforts in multicultural diversity, (b) share learning and experiences, and (c) discuss relevant issues in the management of a culturally diverse organization or team. The conference would also provide an opportunity to recognize and reward visible accountability and progress in managing diversity.

Future Directions

Looking toward the future, DAL has taken several steps to position itself for further progress in tapping the full potential of all employees. A central Diversity Task Force has been set up, with subforces in each department. The objective for each subgroup is to determine what makes sense as next steps. The result should be a laboratorywide plan for advancing managing diversity.

Also, DAL's management has integrated major managing diversity components into general training activities. At one week-long program, a full day is spent on managing diversity. The following topics are covered:

- Historical perspective of diversity within DAL
- Definitions of affirmative action, valuing differences, and managing diversity
- Managing diversity as it relates to acquisitions and mergers
- Managing diversity from an individual perspective

The objective of these components is to foster a mindset that would facilitate implementation of managing diversity.

At least one department has initiated its own diversity education effort, and others are planning possible education initiatives.

These plans address a question that often comes up about managing diversity: Is it legitimate under managing diversity to implement initiatives primarily for the benefit of one group? The answer is yes *if* the conditions in question hold *only* for that particular group. The research study done by DAL demonstrates that groups differ in characteristics and consequently in issues and needs. Therefore, managers are justified in targeting specific objectives.

Two important cautions: Before implementing a "special" intervention for a given group, management must make every effort to ensure that the issue being addressed is valid only for that one group. Otherwise, whatever is done should be targeted toward all groups experiencing the situation. In addition, regardless of how issues vary across groups, managers should seek to address all groups simultaneously through an appropriately varied set of interventions.

DAL's management has done just that. Some of its pioneering activities include the following:

▪ *Improvements in Work/Family Issues.* Building on the results of a corporatewide survey on work/family issues, DAL management has moved to review and liberalize its policies and benefits. For example, it is now possible for employees with family responsibilities to work less than full time.

▪ *Sharpening the Focus on Developmental Candidates.* To ensure that no viable candidates for promotion are overlooked, DAL's management has established three practices.

1. Numerical goals for promotion of women and minorities have been set.
2. Once a year, managers meet and create a development list of minorities and women with upward mobility potential.
3. Once a year senior management meets, discusses, and tracks the experiences and progress of minorities and women.

These practices are designed to enhance the probability that all individuals with proven potential are visible.

▪ *Black Managers' Program.* In response to concerns that black managers were relatively few in number, were experiencing far less upward mobility than other employee groups, and had few role models, DAL instituted a structured program to enhance their development. Essentially, the effort involves a structured career development program for the black manager and a structured cultural awareness program for their managers. A major objective has been to enhance boss-subordinate relationships.

▪ *Black Ph.D. Program.* While black Ph.D.s were among the best educated people in the laboratory, they experienced little upward mobility in the technical hierarchy. This program was launched to enhance their development. Some promotions can in part be attributed to this initiative. Reportedly, black Ph.D.s feel positive about the effort and are enthusiastic about helping increase the number of black Ph.D.s.

The research study by DAL provides an excellent example of a transitional bridge between affirmative action and managing diversity. It simultaneously highlights some key employee differences and reflects the complexity of tapping the full potential of diverse people, while at the same time providing solid evidence of the benefits of doing so and the loss potential of neglecting the task. Perhaps more important, it has been instrumental in "clearing the air" about managing diversity within the entire corporation. The leadership exhibited by DAL's top management serves as an impetus and an example for Culberson's corporate leaders.

Appendix 6A

Interview Questions for Culberson Industries' Research Study

Company selection, retention

1. What attracted you to DAL? How have things measured up to your expectations?
2. What kinds of things have encouraged you to stay with this Company?
3. When you thought about leaving, what was going on?

What has contributed to your success?

4. In what division did you begin your career at DAL?
5. What two or three experiences (events, learnings) have contributed to your success at DAL?
6. What key formal training events have helped you at DAL?
7. During your career, have you had a mentor? [*Define mentor.*] Have you had more than one? What about those experiences that made them rich for you?

Supervision

8. On a scale from 1 to 10, describe the overall quality of supervision and developmental attention [coaching, training, preparation for the next job] that supervisors have provided you?

Assignment

    9. Think about the time when you felt most productive:

        a. What were the qualities of the assignment that helped you feel that way?

        b. What did your supervisor, at that time, do that helped you feel so productive?

Barriers

   10. What key barriers do you feel have worked to hamper your advancement? [*Probe here.*]

Looking to the future

   11. On a scale of 1 to 5, please rate how DAL is doing overall in the area of managing employee diversity.

   12. What issues remain to be addressed to better grow and develop managers in DAL?

       What can be done to improve the addressing of these issues?

   13. What specific steps might be taken to enhance "management of employee diversity" within DAL?

        a. What will it look like?

        b. How do we get there?

        c. How will it help the business?

        d. How will we do it better?

Appendix 6B

Results of Culberson Industries Research Study

Table 6.1. Company Selection and Retention Factors

	All %	White Men %	White Women %	Blacks %	Hispanics %	Asians %
Sign-up Factors						
Nature of the work	50	68	47	29	68	38
People	30	18	37	42	11	43
Security/Stability	29	9	11	29	16	33
Retention Factors						
Nature of the work	50	77	47	33	42	48
Pay benefits	28	32	16	29	37	24
Career opportunities	22	23	47	25	0	14
Family considerations	20	18	0	38	16	24
Company characteristics	15	0	37	0	0	43
Bailout Factors						
Reward/recognition concern	42	36	32	54	42	43
Problem supervisors	42	32	47	33	63	38

Table 6.2. Degree to Which Employee Groups Felt Expectations Met

Blacks	88%
Hispanics	95
Asians/Pacific Islanders	86
White women	90
White men	91

Table 6.3. Factors That Determine Success

	All	White Men	White Women	Blacks	Hispanics	Asians
	%	%	%	%	%	%
Right assignment	68	91	95	75	47	29
Helpful managers	42	50	68	33	47	14
Technical accomplishment	28	0	16	71	0	33
Could work with people	8	0	0	0	37	5

Table 6.4 Mentoring Experiences

	All	White Men	White Women	Blacks	Hispanics	Asians
	%	%	%	%	%	%
Had a mentor?	62	73	89	54	53	43
Had more than one?	43	68	74	29	21	24

Table 6.5. Assessment of Quality of Supervision and Developmental Attention (Scale of 1 to 10)

Blacks	Hispanics	White Women	Asians	White Men
4.1	5.5	6.4	3.7	5.4

Table 6.6. Barriers to Advancement

	All %	White Men %	White Women %	Blacks %	Hispanics %	Asians %
Stereotyping (includes the following three categories)	56	0	74	63	53	95
"Isms"—race, culture, age	25	0	0	46	37	38
Pigeonholed (technology or assignment)	15	0	21	0	0	57
Being female	16	0	53	17	16	0
Lack of training/ development	10	0	0	21	0	29
Communication	8	0	0	0	16	24
Misc. personal factors	7	32	0	0	0	0
Inadequate feedback/ coaching	5	0	26	0	0	0
Management's unease with women	4	0	21	0	0	0
Not into informal network	4	0	21	0	0	0
Difficulty with supervisors	3	14	0	0	0	0
Having to prove myself	3	0	16	0	0	0
Nonsupportive managers	2	0	0	0	11	0
Couldn't change assignments	2	0	0	0	11	0

Chapter 7

Settling in for the Duration—Avon Products, Inc.

Avon's commitment to building a diverse work force had its roots in the affirmative action programs of the 1970s. The company's progress toward its goals has not been smooth or steady. Creating and managing a diverse work force is a process, not a destination.

Since the early 1970s, the company has had clear hiring objectives, a Women and Minority Task Force that reported on issues to senior management, and top management that was consistently supportive. As a result of its aggressive affirmative action programs, Avon has been viewed as a good place for women and minorities to work. Today, Avon has more women officers and directors than any other Fortune 500 company, and nearly 20 percent of its professionals and managers are minorities.

Through the 1970s and well into the 1980s, the company was motivated by a desire "to do the right thing." Like many companies, Avon was operating under the mindset of early civil rights efforts toward integration. It wasn't until the mid-1980s that the company recognized that a changing and segmented marketplace could best be served by a multicultural work force. Once the company recognized that diversity offered competitive advantage, the efforts to build and learn how to manage diversity took on a new dimension. In retrospect, management realized that if the company had better utilized the women in its work force, it could have avoided some of the business problems it encountered in the late 1970s and early 1980s.

Avon was late in responding to the women's movement. Millions of women entering the work force meant fewer women at home to recruit as sales representatives and fewer women at home to sell to. At the same time, Avon's marketplace was becoming more and more diverse. Increasingly its customers included not just suburban housewives, but also a growing number of inner-city residents and minorities.

Marketing research and strategic planning signalled a clear need for Avon to prepare itself to respond to changing consumer demands. Multiculturalism, specifically the valuing differences model, was recognized as an important element in meeting consumer demands and gaining competitive advantage.

The need to stay competitive led to a rethinking of several of Avon's traditional practices, starting with employee selection and promotion. The company, which once promoted almost entirely from within, was now beginning to hire from the outside, particularly at senior levels. This change was related to another: a shift from valuing a generalist background, gained from experience within the company, to valuing expertise in a specialty area.

Senior managers were also concerned about changing facets of the company's culture. They wanted, in particular, to change the company's traditional "nice," nonconfrontational culture to one that candidly addressed performance issues and encouraged risk taking. All this made Avon particularly receptive to the concept of managing diversity.

The Women and Minority Task Force was started in the 1970s to help management understand the issues of women and minorities in the company. In the mid-1980s, the task force evolved into black, Hispanic, and Asian employee networks. The networks serve the company by defining and communicating the cultural aspects of their origins, thereby enhancing the overall culture of the company. In addition, they serve as a support system for members and communicate their issues and concerns to management.

Another indication of the company's interest in more effective management of its diverse work force is its diversity training program. Since the mid-1980s, the company has sent middle-managers with high potential to Morehouse College in Atlanta for a leadership development program designed to broaden their skills in leadership, management, and general business. Avon has also incorporated a managing diversity module in its management training program, focusing strongly on why and how diversity can provide competitive advantage.

Since 1985, Avon's entire management team has participated in awareness training programs provided by outside consultants. The program goes far beyond affirmative action; it focuses on the business advantages of valuing diversity—a recognition of the desirability of mirroring the consumer in the workplace. In 1990 the company reiterated its position on managing diversity by having top management members participate in a strategy and tactic session defining their own positions on managing diversity.

The Multicultural Planning Research Project

Avon's current progress in promoting minorities and women traces back to the mid-1980s, when senior management recognized that it was having much greater success in recruiting minorities and women than it was in having them rise through the ranks. This concerned Avon's executives because it violated their notion of "what was right," and also because it hampered efforts to develop a multicultural work force reflective of a changing marketplace.

A search for the causes led management to commission a consultant-led Multicultural Planning Research Project. The project's goals were to:

1. Identify systems and practices that support or hinder the advancement of minorities and women within Avon.
2. Evaluate the appropriateness of company policies, systems, and practices.
3. Determine employees' and management's perceptions of Avon's promotion practices.

Research methods included the review of Avon's written policies and a series of individual interviews, conducted from July through September 1986. The purpose of the interviews was to "obtain candid perceptions of Avon's policies and practices as they relate to the objectives of the Multicultural Planning Research Project."

Two interview guides were developed: one for senior managers and human resources staff, the other for general management employees who constituted the available pool for promotions (see Appendices 7A and 7B).

Nearly all senior managers were scheduled for interviews. Other participants were chosen by random sampling of employees of minority status and gender. In all, 107 people were interviewed, 50 from corporate headquarters and 57 from several profit-center locations.

Interview questions elicited background career information and comments on:

- How promotions work at Avon
- How employees get feedback on their performance
- The training/developmental opportunities at Avon
- How women were faring in management at Avon
- How minorities were faring in management at Avon
- How multiculturalism would benefit Avon

Management Staffing Practices at Avon

The Recruitment Process. The research indicated that informality characterized the management staffing practices at Avon. Interviewees, for the most part, reported that they had heard of Avon through informal sources. They had joined the organization because of its reputation as a "people-oriented" company and because they were impressed with the treatment they received at the time of their employment interviews. Many mentioned the corporation's position as an industry leader as further enticement for joining.

The Selection and Promotion Process. The same informality that characterized the recruitment process was mirrored in the selection and promotion process. Senior management and human resources did have a process in which managers at different levels engaged in a general discussion about the promotability of lower level candidates. But interviewees perceived their promotability as being controlled primarily by their boss.

Given the informality of the selection and promotion process, a mentor was all important. More than 90 percent of the respondents felt that a mentor was a necessity. Respondents reported not knowing of management openings and complained that "no one knows how to get promoted."

Appraisal and Feedback. The majority of interviewees acknowledged receiving annual performance appraisals, and most felt these were a fair assessment of their performance. Yet the appraisals didn't appear to be tied closely enough to consideration for promotion or career development opportunities. More than half of the respondents, for example, said that compensation was only loosely tied to performance. Senior management interviewees reported that negative feedback had not been a characteristic of Avon's management style.

Development and Training. Career development discussions were perceived as informal and infrequent. Discussions were perceived as inadequate to fill the need for "knowing where [one] stands" in terms of career potential within the company.

Senior managers acknowledged and other interviewees recognized that Avon's traditionally informal training and development system was "behind the times and no longer suited to the challenges Avon now has in the marketplace." More and better management development training was seen as a particular need. Although they were positive about the Morehouse College training experience and one or two other external programs, respondents doubted that outside training services could fill the extent of that need or be specific enough for Avon's needs.

In addition, neither senior managers nor their subordinates were entirely happy with the results of past training initiatives — but for different reasons. Senior managers didn't see enough performance improvement; trainees reported coming back from the sessions feeling they had something to offer but experiencing indifference from their managers.

Women at Avon

Women considered themselves and were considered by others to be "doing okay" at Avon. Numerous women held mid- and low-level management positions. Most frequently cited as key to this success was "the nature of the company and its clients." Yet women at the profit centers perceived themselves and were perceived by others as experiencing barriers to upward mobility within the corporation.

The perception that women lacked a technical background led male interviewees, including some members of senior staff, to conclude that there was "not a large pool of qualified women," and some interviewees felt that the women who were promoted weren't necessarily the most qualified.

Some women saw themselves in a double bind. On the one hand, they felt they had to "work twice as hard to be considered half as good." On the other, they felt they had to accomplish this while being simultaneously "more competent and less threatening."

Lack of Support. All respondents agreed that no special support systems were provided for women and recognized that women were not included in the established male networks. Given the informality of the selection and promotion process, exclusion from these networks created an invisible barrier. Subordinates were dependent on their bosses to make higher-level management aware of their talents. Mid-level managers, in particular, were seen as the least likely to sponsor women.

Chauvinism/Discrimination. The stereotyping of women appeared to have been largely unconscious. Respondents saw gender-related assumptions as preventing men from seeing women as managerial candidates and from perceiving them as peers.

Other Factors. Style, lack of opportunity, and being new to the company were also seen as inhibiting factors. These factors, however, appeared to be less gender- than company-related.

Minorities at Avon

Respondents frequently noted Avon's stated commitment to recruiting, retaining, and promoting minorities. Yet they did not give the company a high rating on its ability to do so. Black males, in particular, were identified as faring the worst under the company's present system. Minorities reported prejudice and discrimination, perceptions of competency, lack of support, style, and lack of opportunity as hindrances.

Prejudice/Discrimination. Respondents reported more open expressions of prejudice/discrimination toward minorities than were reported for women.

Perceptions of Competency. Some minorities were perceived by whites as having been hired or promoted because of their racial characteristics. Black males, in particular, were perceived as "struggling and often held in low regard." The black manager was seen as "modeling failure." On the other hand, minorities themselves felt they had to "be better and try harder" and that they were "judged more harshly."

Lack of Support. Both minority members and their white counterparts recognized a lack of adequate support for minority employees. A white male senior manager said, "We don't do enough to support minorities." Minorities reported that they lacked role models, were not given honest feedback, and did not receive mentoring. The lack of mentoring meant that minorities had no one to sponsor them. They were very aware of this fact. "You need a mentor and it's hard for a minority to get one," said one. "There's not a person I can identify who has said 'Let me help you.'" Another commented, "Maybe I have been sponsored, but I'm not aware of it."

Style. Consistent with other findings about the importance of fitting the Avon mold, style was seen as a significant factor hindering the advancement of minorities. "It's a structured environment requiring you to fit the mold," said one respondent. Black males, in particular, seemed penalized by perceptions of style.

Lack of Opportunity. Lack of opportunity for minorities was seen as being specifically related to minority status. Minority respondents perceived Avon's commitment as being "in numbers rather than substance." Management recognized that, as a result of the lack of upward mobility, too many minorities with management potential were leaving Avon.

Multiculturalism

Multiculturalism was not well understood by many interviewees. Senior managers were much more aware of the term than subordinates, but even some of them were unclear as to its meaning. "I think I understand what it means at a corporate level, and that effective marketing requires effective representation from within," said one respondent. Said another senior manager, "It is important because of the consumer base."

Senior managers who were aware of its significance saw themselves as potential change agents or catalysts. One saw his role as "looking at work performance and not personal characteristics." Another saw her role as being "a nagging little voice to target positions and see that minorities get ahead." Others in the organization, however, envisioned a very passive role: "be a role model," "not feeling prejudice," "be accepting of differences" were typical responses.

Many interviewees expressed a desire to see "more concrete action." And many respondents voiced a desire to see multiculturalism given more importance. Senior management, for example, universally wanted to "put more punch into it. Hold managers accountable, and quantify expectations in multiculturalism more specifically and realistically," they said.

Both senior management and a large majority of respondents wanted to see more effective recruiting and promotion procedures. And a significant number of interviewees reported a sincere desire for cultural information seminars and workshops to facilitate surfacing of and dealing with prejudices and attitudes. Overall, interviewees as a whole signalled a willingness to become more informed and involved in the multicultural arena.

Avon's Responses

Suggestions for several new multicultural initiatives grew out of the Awareness Project. However, as the company was in the process of evaluating them, the top-level decision was made to restructure and downsize the company. As one facet of the reorganization, the division and corporate affirmative action functions were consolidated, and multiculturalism was delegated to the divisions.

Then, in a second reorganization, responsibility for multiculturalism was moved from the division level down to various regions and branches. In the process, the commitment to multiculturalism lost some of its momentum. Even though senior management was committed, this commitment had not had time to penetrate the lower levels.

Throughout this time, however, the minority networks were encouraged to operate. Their existence helped keep multiculturalism alive.

Renewed Commitment

In early 1990, Avon renewed its commitment to diversity. The responsibility for monitoring multiculturalism progress was returned to the corporate vice-president of human resources, but multiculturalism continues to be a responsibility of line organizations.

Task Force on Managing Diversity

The corporation created a task force on managing diversity and charged it with very specific responsibilities:

- Define a diverse work force.
- Determine the value of managing diversity effectively and achieving a diverse work force.
- Analyze Avon's work force issues.
- Recommend actions directed at more effective management of diversity.

Definition of Diversity. Significantly, the task force decided that all of the employees who were affected by Avon's staff development process were "diverse" enough to fall under its purview. This included, of course, minorities and women.

The task force observed also that gay males may have "fit" problems similar to those of minorities and may require flexibility in benefits programs. And they included religious minorities, employees over age 40, and the handicapped among the diverse. "Diversity is not," the task force concluded, "a question of race."

Benefits of Effectively Addressing Diversity. A business payoff was cited as the most important benefit of managing diversity. Task force members suggested that the successful management of diversity could allow Avon to become the beauty company of choice both for consumers and for able employees regardless of race or gender. They also predicted that recruitment would be easier and that training and development would have a greater payoff as turnover was reduced. In addition, they believed that the added empowerment and enablement of all employees would become increasingly essential as Avon's search for efficiency and effectiveness created a flatter and smaller organization.

Current Work Force Issues. As a part of their deliberations, task force members conducted a limited number of interviews to determine issues. They found all interviewees concerned that the staff development process was not effective enough. They also found that black men and Hispanics perceived their position and opportunities in the company much as they had in 1986. They found Asian Americans clustered in staff departments.

Most changed were women's perceptions. Their previous concerns about stereotyping and sexism had waned as more women had ascended to the ranks of senior management. The concern had shifted to caretaker-related benefits such as expanded maternity benefits, child care, elder care, flextime, and job sharing.

Task Force Recommendations. The task force recommended both easily implemented, short-term solutions and more complex, long-term solutions. They emphasized education designed to make all managers aware of the corporation's commitment to managing diversity and the business reasons for this commitment. Recommendations for improving Avon's staff development process contain items that, when implemented, will affect the organization's culture. For example, they suggested setting and communicating objective, specific performance criteria, evaluating employees' performance, and providing candid feedback about performance. Members placed special urgency on immediate improvement of the development process for high-potential and minority people, and recommended specific actions to facilitate this goal.

Human Resources Strategy and a Five-Year Implementation Plan

Equally significant to Avon's commitment to managing diversity is the development of a new human resources strategy and five-year implementation plan. First and foremost, this plan is one for changing culture.

It demonstrates how concrete action steps can be associated with efforts to create a culture supportive of managing diversity. For this reason, the complete plan is included as Appendix 7C.

A key feature of this plan is its assumption that it can be implemented only through a partnership between human resources and line management. Plan components include both current and five-year goals for:

- Getting the right people in the right place
- Keeping people informed of the company's values, visions, expectations, and actions
- Reinforcing and rewarding performance
- Providing career planning and training and development to help people grow
- Integrating work and family policies and programs to offer more flexible and appropriate benefits
- Identifying and managing diversity through programs, informed mentoring initiatives, and accountability for managers

Key to the development programs, for example, is manager training in appropriate confrontation and counseling. Key to the lasting corporate change are efforts to institutionalize and integrate initiatives related to managing diversity.

Settling in for the Duration

Avon is now where its managers would have liked to be five years ago. The current plan may be a delayed response, but this type of delay is not uncommon with long-term change. Indeed, Avon's experiences to date illustrate a typical scenario that accompanies change efforts of this magnitude. The work of Avon's task force and human resources department has resulted in a quality set of recommendations and plans.

While Avon now is positioned to move forward, it still will experience on and off periods—simply because of the nature and time frame of the change effort. Its managers and employees will have to settle in for the duration with sufficient patience and perseverance.

The task force's conclusions and recommendations indicate more than a name change from multiculturalism to managing diversity. They indicate a maturing of the company's perspective as well.

One of the most significant task force conclusions is that diversity includes *everybody* and is not defined simply by gender and race. This understanding gives members a willingness to stand on their conviction that a commitment to diversity is a commitment to all employees, not an attempt at preferential treatment.

Equally significant is the task force's identification of managing diversity as a *business issue*. This is particularly important because earlier beliefs that employee diversity was a social responsibility concern were not sufficient to garner continued commitment when the company went through turbulent times.

Finally, the task force's recommendations that specific actions be taken to develop minority employees in the interim while managing diversity is put into place, indicates a realistic assessment of the time, effort, and commitment that the managing diversity initiative will take. It represents, in short, a recognition that a 104-year-old culture won't change without considerable vision, leadership, and expenditure of time.

The five-year plan developed by the human resources department is notable for its movement toward a management philosophy of employee empowerment. In addition, it incorporates the understanding that managing diversity is a business issue. Perhaps most significant, it places the company in a position to adopt the "we are team" as opposed to "we are family" cultural root. Because such a root assumes that only performance is needed for inclusion, it promises to enhance Avon's ability to meet its human resources goals.

Appendix 7A

Avon's Interview Guide for Senior Management and Human Resources Staff

I. Background/Career: Tell me about your career.

   1. Tell me about your career at Avon.

      — Specific positions.
      — Length of time in positions.
      — Which were promotions and which were broadening?
      — Describe your current job and major responsibilities.
      — What did you do prior to Avon?

   2. What usually attracts people to Avon?

   3. What initially attracted you to Avon?

      — Were your expectations met?
      — Have your expectations changed?

   4. How would you compare your workload when you first started at your present position with your current situation? How prepared did you feel when you started at your current position and how prepared do you feel now?

II. Promotional Opportunities: How do promotions work at Avon?

    5. How do employees find out about job openings at management levels?

    6. What does it take to be promoted at Avon?

       — What types of people get ahead at Avon?
       — Is there a shortage or surplus of good candidates within Avon for management level positions?
       — What is Avon's promotion policy?
       — What changes would you make in promotion policy?

    7. Are mentors important for career progress at Avon?

       — Have you had a mentor during your career at Avon?

    8. In promotion to management, what use, if any, is made of the following selection tools:

       — Interviews
       — Formal appraisals
       — Testing
       — Self-nomination
       — Group judgment of higher management potential

    In promotion to management, what use, if any, is made of the following indices:

       — Performance in training
       — Objective measures of job performance
       — Seniority
       — Protected group status
       — Probationary period on the job
       — Educational background
       — Style
       — Readiness

    9. When hiring from the outside at the manager level what use is made of the following:

- Interviews
- Testing
- Recommendations
- Educational background
- Experience
- Affirmative action

10. Is there a shortage or surplus of good candidates within Avon for management level positions?

11. Is there a shortage or surplus of good external candidates for Avon management positions? Why?

III. Performance Feedback: How do employees at Avon get feedback on their performance?

12. How often are performance appraisals conducted?

- How are performance appraisals used?
- Are they looked at to identify potential?
- What emphasis is placed on career development?

13. Is compensation tied to performance appraisals? If not, to what?

- Are people paid what they're worth?
- Is performance a factor in compensation?
- How?

IV. Training and Development: How do you feel about the training and/or developmental opportunities at Avon?

14. Is training provided to management-potential employees?

- Is additional training available for those who want it?

V. Opportunities for Women: How are women doing in management here at Avon?

15. What special opportunities does Avon provide for women in management positions?

    — Do women need additional or special opportunity programs? Why? What types?

16. What do you see as Avon's commitment to women in management positions?

    —Give me an example.

17. Do you feel that women with management potential are leaving Avon?

    — Why are they leaving?

18. How do you feel women are viewed in relation to their skills as managers?

    — As directors or officers?
    — Their potential as managers?
    — As directors or officers?

19. Should there be special training programs for women?

20. Is there a shortage or surplus of good women candidates within Avon for management level positions?

21. How successful are women selected for Avon management positions?

22. Do you feel that many women hired from the outside for Avon management positions who perform satisfactorily or better leave of their own volition?

23. What factors facilitate the advancement of women at Avon?

24. What factors hinder the advancement of women at Avon?

25. What could Avon do to make the company a better place for women managers to work?

26. What is your perception of Avon vis-à-vis other companies regarding the climate for women in management?

VI. Opportunities for Minorities: How are minorities doing in management here at Avon?

27. What special opportunities does Avon provide for minorities in management positions?

    — Do minorities need additional or special opportunities? Why? What types?

28. What do you see as Avon's commitment to minorities in management positions?

    — Give an example.

29. Do you feel that minorities with management potential are leaving Avon?

    — Why are they leaving?

30. How do you feel minorities are viewed in relation to their skills as managers?

    — As directors or officers?
    — Their potential as managers?
    — As directors or officers?

31. Should there be special training programs for minorities?

32. Is there a shortage or surplus of good minority candidates within Avon for management level positions?

33. How successful are minorities selected for Avon management positions?

34. Do you feel that many minorities hired from the outside for Avon management positions who perform satisfactorily or better leave of their own volition?

35. What factors facilitate the advancement of minorities at Avon?

36. What factors hinder the advancement of minorities at Avon?

37. What could Avon do to make the company a better place for minority managers to work?

38. What is your perception of Avon vis-à-vis other companies regarding the climate for minorities in management?

VII. Multiculturalism: We have heard a lot about Avon's commitment to a multicultural work force. (Multicultural means "people of diverse race, sex, and culture.") How will multiculturalism benefit the company?

39. What do you see as your role in building a multicultural work force?

40. What do you need to be a more effective manager of a multicultural work force?

41. Are there any unique aspects to working with women?

   — With minorities?

42. What advice would you give young women interested in management at Avon?

   — Young minorities?

Appendix 7B

Avon's Interview Guide for Manager Level and Below

I. Background/career: Tell me about your career.

1. Tell me about your career at Avon.

    — Specific positions.
    — Length of time in positions.
    — Which were promotions and which were broadening?
    — Describe your current job and major responsibilities.
    — What did you do prior to Avon?

2. What usually attracts people to Avon?

3. What initially attracted you to Avon?

    — Were your expectations met?
    — Have your expectations changed?

4. What do you see as your "next step" at Avon?

    — Where do you think you will be in five years?
    — Where do you think you will be in ten years?

5. What future positions at Avon would you like?

    — What would help you get these positions?
    — Does anything stand in the way?

6. How would you compare your workload when you first started at your present position with your current situation?

   — How prepared did you feel when you started at your current position?
   — How prepared do you feel now?

II. Promotional Opportunities: How do promotions work at Avon?

7. How do you find out about job openings at management levels?

8. What do you think it takes to be promoted at Avon?

   — What types of people get ahead at Avon?
   — Do people who are promoted really deserve it?
   — Is there a shortage or surplus of good candidates within Avon for management level positions?
   — What is your understanding of Avon's promotion policy?
   — What changes would you make in Avon's promotion policy?

9. Have you progressed as rapidly as you think you should?

10. What promotional opportunities have you had at Avon?

    — Why do you believe you were promoted?

11. What promotion opportunities have you tried for but didn't get?

    — Why do you believe the other persons were selected?
    — Why do you believe you were not promoted?

12. What promotional opportunities have you wanted but didn't try for?

    — Why didn't you try?

13. Are mentors important for career progress at Avon?

     — Have you had a mentor during your career at Avon?

     — Describe your relationship with this person.

III. Performance Feedback: How do you get feedback on your performance?

    14. How often do you receive feedback?

    15. When did you last receive a performance appraisal?

       — Do you feel it is an accurate assessment of your performance?

       — What emphasis is placed on career development?

    16. Is compensation tied to performance appraisals?

       — Are people paid what they are worth?

IV. Training and Development: How do you feel about the training and/or developmental opportunities at Avon?

    17. Do you know if a developmental plan has been made for you?

       — Is training provided to management-potential employees?

       — Is additional training available for those who want it?

V. Opportunities for Women: How are women doing in management here at Avon?

    18. Do you feel that women with management potential are leaving Avon?

       — Why are they leaving?

    19. How far up the management ladder do you think women can go in Avon?

— Why?
— Is there a shortage or surplus of good women candidates within Avon for management level positions?

20. What do you see as Avon's commitment to women in management positions?

21. What opportunities does Avon provide for women in management positions?

22. What factors facilitate the advancement of women here at Avon?

23. What factors hinder the advancement of women here at Avon?

24. What is your perception of Avon vis-à-vis other companies regarding the climate for women in management?

VI. Opportunities for Minorities: How are minorities doing in management here at Avon?

25. Do you feel that minorities with management potential are leaving Avon?

— Why are they leaving?

26. How far up the management ladder do you think minorities can go in Avon?

— Why?
— Is there a shortage or surplus of good candidates within Avon for management level positions?

27. What do you see as Avon's commitment to minorities in management positions?

28. What opportunities does Avon provide for minorities in management positions?

29. What factors facilitate the advancement of minorities here at Avon?

30. What factors hinder the advancement of minorities here at Avon?

31. What is your perception of Avon vis-à-vis other companies regarding the climate for minorities in management?

VII. Multiculturalism: We have heard a lot about Avon's commitment to a multicultural work force. (Multicultural means "people of diverse race, sex, and culture.") How will multiculturalism benefit the company?

32. What do you see as your role in building a multicultural work force?

33. What do you need to be a more effective manager of a multicultural work force?

34. Are there any unique aspects to working with women?

    — With minorities?

35. What advice would you give young women interested in management at Avon?

    — Young minorities?

Appendix 7C.

Avon's Human Resource Strategy and Five-Year Implementation Plan

1995 Objectives

- A company noted for the competency of its people, and for helping its people develop their full potential.
- A company in which each associate acts as though she/he is totally responsible for their relationships and results created.
- A company disciplined in its management processes: performance review, human resources review, objective setting, career developing. People know where they stand. People are helped to assess their strengths and their development needs and are provided with the resources to satisfy those needs.
- The number one company in the world in managing diversity.
- A company with a compensation philosophy closely aligned to its strategies. Compensation programs tailored to specific needs within the organization, and designed to give the highest rewards to people who make the biggest contributions.
- A company that has been experimental and adventuresome in designing flexible work schedules that meet the needs of its diverse work force.
- Finally, a company that has been successful in eliminating layers in the organization, instilling teamwork across functions, and empowering decision making to occur close to the customer.

A Need to Change the Culture

Where We Are Today	*Where We Need to Go*
Employment security. Associates think of themselves only in relation to Avon. They think in terms of entitlement, and not in terms of relative contribution.	*Employment security.* Associates who contribute and learn most increase their value in both the internal and external labor markets. (Requires: projects that offer challenge, growth, and provide credit for results.)
Fairness equals treating people the same. "Cookie cutter" approach.	*Fairness equals treating people appropriately.* Differentiated approach.
Being liked. This often leads to not telling the truth. Weakness in confrontation/coaching skills compounds this issue.	*Being respected by all.* Telling the truth, being open, candid with people.
Preoccupation with playing the game. Emphasis on looking good, looking up, pleasing, on career development. Accomplishing someone else's goals.	*Preoccupation with learning and assuming responsibility.* Open landscape, developing own sense of purpose, accepting responsibility for relationships and results.
Decisions made at high levels in organization.	*Empowered associates making decisions at lower levels in the organization.*
Leadership roles reserved for senior leaders.	*Self-leaders at all levels who assume as much responsibility as possible and strive to become capable of assuming more.*
Lack of cooperation/coordination across functions.	*Culture built on cooperation, teamwork, and cross-functional alliances.*

> This is a major systemic change in thinking and working that requires a partnership between human resources and line management, a disciplined expression of our values, and a commitment to helping associates achieve "employability security."

The Challenge

- The change will be dramatic and different.
- It has the potential to disorient our people.
- As we go through the change, we must counter disorientation with as much information and support as possible.
- Training in coaching, counseling, and confronting issues.
- Clearer communication of purpose, missions, and results.
- Results-driven structures.

Requirement for Achievement of Our Vision

Excellence in both management and leadership skills must be maintained at a high level and both sets of skills must be focused on ensuring that human resources policies and practices:

- Are congruent with Avon's values and vision of what it wants to be.
- Are integrated with Avon's operating goals and strategies.
- Reflect in their treatment of associates the way Avon wants associates to treat their customers.
- Provide recognition and rewards for learning, growing, and assuming responsibility for results.
- Provide compensation for associates that is determined by both financial results and demonstration of self-leadership and teamwork.
- Are supported by results-driven structures and information systems.

Human Resources Strategy: Integration of Six Major Components

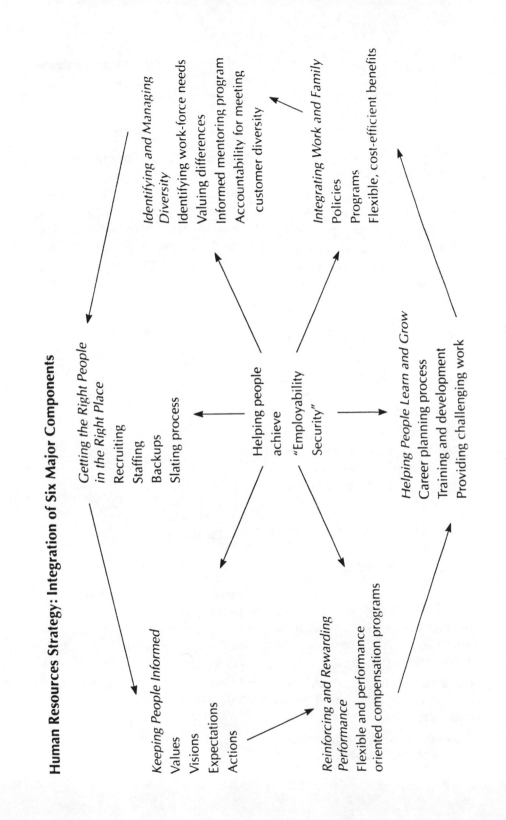

Getting the Right People in the Right Place
Recruiting
Staffing
Backups
Slating process

Keeping People Informed
Values
Visions
Expectations
Actions

Reinforcing and Rewarding Performance
Flexible and performance oriented compensation programs

Helping people achieve "Employability Security"

Identifying and Managing Diversity
Identifying work-force needs
Valuing differences
Informed mentoring program
Accountability for meeting customer diversity

Integrating Work and Family
Policies
Programs
Flexible, cost-efficient benefits

Helping People Learn and Grow
Career planning process
Training and development
Providing challenging work

Getting the Right People in the Right Place

Current Plan

Identify external sources to provide skills/diversity needed.

Establish local career days, job fairs, a central network for recruiting, college recruiting, summer intern programs, professional networks for women/minorities, high school cooperatives.

Develop network for loan/sabbatical opportunities at selected institutions.

Use Human Resources/Succession Plan to identify backups for key positions.

Implement slating process that includes flexibility to accommodate developmental needs in meeting position requirements.

By 1995

Results-driven organizational and staffing strategies to achieve the necessary skill requirements, cultural compatibility and diversity expectations. Line management will institutionalize and execute strategies.

Reinforcing and Rewarding Performance

Current Plan

Determine performance-oriented plans and develop a more flexible compensation and benefit approach in response to achievement of plans.

Develop linkages between compensation plans and management plans.

Explore ways of compensating team accomplishments in ways

By 1995

Have in place a flexible, competitive compensation program that attracts and retains a qualified, diverse work force. Also have in place management practices and work systems that provide motivation and reinforcement for both team and individual accomplishments.

that encourage associates to perform as both functional and cross-functional team members.

Keeping People Informed

Current Plan

Communicate plans, expectations, and requirements that pertain to human resources activities related to Avon's vision.

Use change processes that help associates at all levels align their own sense of purpose with this vision.

By 1995

Associates will be talking and living the vision by having developed their own, aligned sense of purpose. A climate of trust, respect, and full disclosure will encourage people to confront issues that get in the way of living the vision and achieving its purpose.

Helping People Learn and Grow

Current Plan

Conduct Performance Management Process (PMP) training based on qualitative audit and by request.

Prepare procedure guide for career development system.

Enhance core curriculum.

Utilize more fully tuition reimbursement.

Provide training to support managers in balancing job challenges with skill levels while continually raising the expectations of excellence.

By 1995

Have a comprehensive PMP and career development system in place, with managers trained in coaching, counseling, confrontation, and other relative skills. Associates will participate fully in setting work objectives derived from business requirements, their own sense of purpose, and Avon's vision. Each associate will assume responsibility for actively planning and creating development opportunities for herself or for himself.

Integrating Work and Family

Current Plans

Develop a flexible benefits program.

Define and pilot new policies: reduced work week, work at home, job sharing, flexible hours.

Review maternity leave, and design adoption and family leave policies, sabbaticals.

Plan needs analysis and hold meetings on child/elder care issues across all locations.

By 1995

Support and meet the broad and diverse needs of the future work force through benefit plans, policies and programs that create an environment that allows for balance between work and family for all associates.

Identifying and Managing Diversity

Current Plans

Review organizations for diversity in relation to current and projected demographics of labor force and customers.

Help organizations develop goals and accountability.

Provide diversity awareness training and education for officers, directors, managers.

Include in new-hire orientation.

Integrate with Avon Foundation.

Reevaluate Participation Council.

By 1995

Have in place organization in which the diversity of the workplace reflects the realities of the labor force and our customer base. Role models for all elements of the diverse workplace will abound and the work culture will support and secure diversity and the management of diversity.

Outcome

A highly productive workplace that has meaning, dignity, and a sense of community and in which people can realistically develop a reasonable measure of "employability security" for themselves.

ACTION STEPS, AVON HUMAN RESOURCES PLAN

HR Action Plan Milestones

	1990	1991	1992	1993	1994	1995
Communication						
Officer, director buy-in to vision action steps, expectations, requirements.	X					
Communicate HR action plans for 1990 to all associates.	X					
Ongoing written, verbal communication on action plan, steps and expectations to all associates.		X	X	X	X	X
Career Development						
Annual PMP's complete/objectives set	X	X	X	X	X	X
Career development plans/skill inventory system for all locations	X					
High Potential		X				
Directors			X			
Managers				X		
Supervisors					X	
All-exempt; high-potential nonexempt						X

Core Curriculum						
Enhanced	X					
Director/manager high potentials/new-hires		X				
Director group/new-hires (half)			X			
Managers/directors/new-hires (half)				X		
Supervisors/directors/new-hires (half)					X	
All director/managers/supervisors completed						X
HR Review						
Directors	X					
High-potential managers		X				
Managers			X			
All supervisors; high-potential exempt				X		
All exempt; high-potential nonexempt					X	
Qualified associates with backups at all levels						X
Recruiting/Staffing						
External sources to support skill/diversity needs	X					
Establish college recruiting, summer intern programs, etc.		X				
College loan/sabbatical pilot			X			
College loan/sabbatical based on evaluation					X	X
Comprehensive network to recruit						X

HR Action Plan Milestones

	1990	1991	1992	1993	1994	1995
Diversity						
Review diversity by organization and set goals:	X					
Action steps to attain goals		X	X	X	X	
Attainment of diversity goals						X
Diversity Program						
Officers/directors	X	X				
Managers/supervisors/new-hires			X	X	X	
All associates						X
Work and Family						
Research needs for:						
Flex Benefits feasibility review	X	X				
Based on evaluation, plan and design			X			
Communicate and enroll				X	X	
Implement						X

Define policies, leaves and child/elder programs; determine assessment	X					
Assess headquarters; pilot policies, child/elder care programs		X				
Assess pilot policies, child/elder programs in locations and implement in headquarters			X			
Implement in locations			X			
Fully implement nationally				X	X	X
Compensation and Benefits						
Develop compensation tie-in to management plan	X					
Phase in plan with defined goals			X	X	X	
Compensation plan fully in place						X
Gain sharing/profit sharing						
Design	X	X				
Implementation	X	X				
Philosophy review and communication						
Review						
Communication						

Action Steps, June–December 1990

Communication	Responsibility
Communicate vision, plan expectations and requirements, change process, tie-in of HR pieces	HR
Obtain officer and director buy-in	HR
Take to all exempt and nonexempt	HR/Officers/Directors

Career Development	
Complete annual PMP's and objectives for all associates	Officers/Dirs/Mgrs/Supvs
Conduct PMP training based on qualitative audit and by request	HR
Determine career development system and skills inventory software	HR
Enhance core curriculum	HR
Complete HR review/succession plan through directors	HR/Management
Position description questionnaires	HR

Recruiting and Staffing	
Identify external resources: skills qualifications to support diversity	HR
Implement slating process	HR/Management

By 1995

Communication	Responsibility
Talking and living the vision	All associates
Have all HR components fully integrated and operative	All associates

Career Development	
Complete 100% of annual PMP's/ objective setting for all associates	Supervisors and above

Compete PMP training and require for new-hires, supervisors and above	HR
Have career development/skills inventory in place for all exempts and high-potential nonexempts	HR/Management
Complete core curriculum and link to levels (required for all new-hires)	HR/Management
Complete HR review and succession plan at all levels with identified backups	HR/Management
Institutionalized Resource Center	HR

Diversity

Review each organization for diversity and determine goals, timing	HR/Management/Networks
Reinstitute Open Door	HR/Management
Provide diversity awareness and education for officers, directors, managers	HR/Management
Include in new-hire orientation	HR/Management

Work and Family

Initiate feasibility study for flexible benefits	HR
Define and pilot new policies: reduced work week, work at home, job sharing	HR/Management
Review maternity leave and design adoption and family leave policies, sabbaticals	HR
Plan needs analysis on child/elder care issues across all locations	HR/Management

Compensation and Benefits

Develop strategy to tie compensation to management plan and receive officer and director buy-in	HR/Management
Develop gain sharing design/communication	HR/Management
Review and communicate compensation philosophy to all associates	HR/Management
Update all survey data and review salary levels as appropriate	HR/Management

Recruiting and Staffing

Institutionalize recruiting and staffing
strategies to meet skill requirements and
assure diversity   HR

Diversity

Have in place organizations in which
associates represent and support a
multiplicity of diversity   All associates

Work and Family

Support and meet the broad and diverse
needs of the future work force through
plans, programs, and policies   HR/Management
Support the balance of work and family for
all associates through plans, programs,
and policies   HR/Management

Compensation and Benefits

Have in place a flexible/competitive
compensation/benefits plan that attracts
and retains a qualified, diverse work
force   HR/Management

Chapter 8

Managing Diversity and Total Quality: An Integrated Strategy for Organizational Renewal

In an increasingly competitive environment, many of America's corporations are engaged in a variety of efforts to renew their enterprises: visioning, thinking strategically, building and changing corporate culture, downsizing, and, most recently, total quality—an initiative that emphasizes the importance of participatory decision making and high-performance work teams. Managing diversity now explicitly joins the list, although it has always been implicitly a part of the renewal effort. Much of what executives are now doing in their search for enhanced viability implicitly requires a managing diversity capability.

The point to remember is that these various approaches are related, and that one paves the way for the others. This is especially true when we look at managing diversity in relation to total quality. Together, they constitute an integral strategy for renewal.

What Is Total Quality?

Total quality is one of the most promising new ideas in the continuing efforts to maximize employee productivity and restore American competitiveness. Most managers would agree that it can be traced to Dr. W. Edwards Deming's work with Japanese industrialists over a period of some thirty years.[1] They disagree on exactly what it involves.

Some managers see total quality as a collection of techniques: quality circles, just-in-time inventory control, employee suggestion systems, participatory management, and continuous improvement. Others see it as a collection of principles: managerial commitment and involvement, dedication to customers, employee involvement, and improved processes.[2]

A broader view holds that total quality is a comprehensive approach calling for a change in the very fabric of the American corporation. Managers who hold this perspective contend that total quality represents, at heart, a cultural change. That means it takes more than trying out some techniques or adopting a set of principles. It demands modifying the fundamental assumptions that control U.S. businesses.

This broader view has been well described by Andrea Gabor:

> While many companies have come to understand that they must conduct their businesses differently, few have grasped the enormity of the task that faces them. Some companies adopt SPC [statistical process control] in their manufacturing operations only to discover that marketing and sales have been left out of the improvement loop. . . . Yet other companies spend millions retraining their workers, but neglect to educate managers about their new role in the process. Quality management, Deming style, is a holistic philosophy that must be adopted in its entirety if it is to work at all.[3]

American Managers Experience Total Quality

Typically, managers' perspectives on total quality evolve over time as their experience with it grows. First they are fascinated and preoccupied with the mechanics. It takes a while before they recognize that what they are doing is really a cultural or "fabric" change—far beyond the mechanics. A quality manager described his company's progression:

We were busy with the mechanics of quality. At this point, we were doing the business *and* quality. There was no integration. We were getting results by doing quality and then going to manage the business.

We needed quality goals that led to business success, and business goals that led to quality success. We needed to integrate business and quality.[4]

Impressive results can be achieved during the mechanical stage, as various "success" stories have shown. Yet successes achieved during this stage can prove to be elusive, or extremely difficult to sustain.

Managers faced with this reality have several choices:

1. Recommit to the same or additional total quality techniques.
2. Adjust their aspirations downward.
3. Reject total quality as unworkable.
4. Expand their understanding of the concept of quality.

Managers who recommit must first rethink their resolve. After reexamining their rationale for moving forward and finding it adequate, they turn to the specifics of the task. "Why," they ask, "aren't we getting the desired results? What are we doing wrong?" Typically, they refine their implementation strategies.

Managers who are less enthusiastic may adjust their aspirations downward. These managers aren't ready to discount quality, but they believe they've achieved what is reasonable, given their company's characteristics and the nature of the effort. So they adopt a piecemeal approach. Some, for example, eliminate the name but keep part of the concept. In this context, some use task forces that operate sporadically to solve specific problems (usually posed by management). Other companies create all-encompassing employee involvement programs characterized by mandatory participation. Only a few retain the comprehensive notion of total quality as popularized in Japan.

Reasons for rejection of total quality range from ineffective management to perceived cultural incompatibility. One quality circle pioneer, for example, failed to weave the motivation for and commitment to the circles into its fabric. The result: the circles were abandoned after the departure of one of its first quality leaders.[5] Other companies have discontinued quality techniques after deciding that they are not compatible with American culture. Success with the techniques, they believe, requires such "Japanese" practices as minimizing the differences in how managers and workers are treated, and fostering job longevity. "That's all well and good for the Japanese," they say, "but Americans just don't think that way."

Managers who have been most successful with total quality are those who, after reexamining their successes, have decided to broaden the concept. Total quality becomes for them not a technique but a comprehensive management philosophy. These managers take a leadership role. They become change agents, not just advocates of a program.

Remaining Challenges

Some of these managers, however, have discovered that even this is not enough. Total quality's effects remain beneficial, but the benefits begin to plateau as the amount of energy needed to maintain a given level of progress increases. This reality is typical of managerial efforts that don't incorporate consideration of the corporation's core assumptions. It represents the Achilles heel of total quality. Even winners of the prestigious Malcolm Baldrige Prize, for example, haven't achieved holistic total quality. Contenders are judged, instead, on progress with individual quality techniques, and on the intensity and extent of their efforts *toward* comprehensive implementation. Little, if any, attention is given to whether root cultural assumptions have been unearthed and made congruent with total quality.

This, of course, explains the difficulty in providing "proof" of the link between performance and total quality. Certainly, a business case can be made for progress with selected total quality techniques. But belief that adopting a holistic approach to total quality will pay off still requires leaps of vision and logic, since no company has achieved this level of implementation.

That doesn't mean that the case is implicitly weak. But doer managers with tunnel vision and short-term time frames often have trouble relating to arguments based on vision and logic.

Even managers with broad vision and open minds are concerned about the difficulty of changing core corporate assumptions (roots). They are increasingly eager to explore ways total quality can be integrated with other change-oriented initiatives. And that brings us to managing diversity.

Integrating Total Quality and Managing Diversity

Individually, both total quality and managing diversity offer potential for enhancing corporate competitiveness, and both face challenges that inhibit their implementation. When the two are used in combination, the challenges are better managed and the benefits are increased—synergy at its best.

Total quality and managing diversity are similar in perspective and in intent. But they are not equally well understood. Practitioners may argue about the scope of total quality, but they generally agree on what it is. Not so with managing diversity. Many not only fail to differentiate among affirmative action, valuing differences, and managing diversity; they use such terms as "multiculturalism," "diversity," and "pluralism" with imprecision as well. The result is conceptual confusion. Total quality's skills and techniques are also more advanced than those of managing diversity. Yet their commonalities are more significant.

■ *Both efforts are grounded in business rationales.* Managers who become excited about total quality and managing diversity are motivated by competitive realities. Corning, Inc.'s experience is an example. In the early 1980s, this company, faced with aggressive competition, reduced profits, and an assertive work force, decided to adopt a total quality initiative. The Corning Quality Management System was developed and a Quality Institute established. Over the years, this participatory effort has shifted in focus but remains true to its goals. Corning managers are excited about the results and have made substantial progress.[6]

Managers serious about implementing managing diversity

are attracted by the same kind of reasoning. They see managing diversity as a strategy for competitiveness. Jim Preston, CEO of Avon Products, says:

> Some people say that by 1995, three out of four people coming into the workplace will be women or minorities. That is a fact. Well, if you are going to attract the best of those people into your organization, you'd better have a culture; you'd better have an environment in which those people feel they can prosper and flourish. If you don't they will go elsewhere and you'll be at a competitive disadvantage.
>
> This is not some type of benevolent activity on our part. There is self-interest here. We have to have a culture and environment in which these people can flourish, and that's what we are working toward.[7]

- *Both total quality and managing diversity stress empowerment or involvement of employees.* Total quality requires that people be fully involved and committed; managing diversity calls for the empowerment of people who are diverse. This means that *managing diversity is a prerequisite* for full implementation of total quality. In an increasingly diverse work force, total quality's emphasis on empowering people translates into our definition of managing diversity—empowering people who are diverse.

Progressive organizations are beginning to acknowledge this interrelationship. Their managers realize that if total quality is a priority item, managing diversity is also. If total quality is strategic and competitive, managing diversity is too, since total quality requires managing diversity capability.

- *Both total quality and managing diversity represent "way of life" changes.* Implementation requirements for both options are so broad and deep that they require fundamental changes in the way corporations do business. Deming comments on the magnitude of the challenge:

> Even when the management of a company embarks in earnest on the fourteen points for quality, production, and competitive position, advancement will at best ap-

pear to be sluggish. One must allow five years for the purchasing department to learn their new job. . . .

Companies with good management will require five years to remove the barriers that make it impossible for the worker to take pride in his work. Many companies will require ten years. . . .

It may be obvious to anyone . . . that a long thorny road lies ahead in American Industry—ten to thirty years . . .[8]

• *Both require cultural changes for full implementation.* Established corporations are highly unlikely to be able to implement either managing diversity or total quality fully without cultural root change. It isn't that they can't secure behavioral change; this can be done by decree, if necessary. The problem is that if behavioral changes are incongruent with the corporation's roots (culture), they will be short-lived—a painful reality for managers familiar with the start-and-stop process of major change initiatives.

Sustainable, long-term *natural* behavioral change requires congruence with the organization's roots. If the culture does not support the desired behavioral change, the culture must be modified. Managers who drive behavioral change on the assumption that the roots will follow are doomed to repeat the cycle. When they relax their efforts they find the oak root saying to the grafted peach limb, "This is *still* an *oak* tree."

• *Both total quality and managing diversity require long-term, pioneering change.* Most managers have little experience with the false starts, ups and downs, ambiguities, uncertainties, and ambivalences that characterize such change. And most of them are uncomfortable with pioneering. That's why they ask this tell-tale question: "Can you tell us about the successes of other companies with managing diversity?"

When managing diversity is integrated with total quality, the most significant implementation challenges that remain with total quality are more successfully addressed. This integration also addresses another important issue: manager overload and the fragmentation that can occur as a result of too many unrelated initiatives. Any new and complex approach takes time and effort. Implementing managing diversity within the context of total quality gives managers and employees a sense of continuity and unified purpose.

Such integration is, however, more successful if the two thrusts are seen as connected but *separate*. This is particularly true when a relatively well-established initiative such as total quality is paired with a more recent one such as managing diversity.

As American businesses struggle with their overall renewal agenda, appropriate integration between total quality and managing diversity can make the difference between success and failure.

Chapter 9

Questions and Answers for Managers

Because managing diversity is on the leading edge of thinking about human resource management, and because implementing it is complex, there are many questions and many misconceptions. Particularly difficult for many is separating managing diversity's general assumptions from those of affirmative action and valuing differences.

Some wonder about securing commitment from senior management, others about the pragmatics of initiating such a complex venture. In this chapter are some of the most frequently asked questions about managing diversity.

Question: Briefly, how would you define managing diversity?

Answer: Managing diversity is a holistic approach to creating a corporate environment that allows all kinds of people to reach their full potential in pursuit of corporate objectives. It is *not* a prepackaged set of solutions. It is *not* a program for addressing discrimination.

Question: What was the motivation for creating managing diversity? Was it an effort to get away from the negative images associated with affirmative action, such as quotas and unqualified people?

Answer: This may be a byproduct of managing diversity, but it was not its driving force. Managing diversity is not a ruse for "backdooring" affirmative action. It approaches diversity from a management perspective: how best to manage the company's human resources, given the fact that those resources are now far more diverse than in earlier times. It is not about leveling the playing field to give minorities and women an extra advantage; it's about maximizing the contributions of *all* employees. It is something that is done for the benefit of the corporation in the interests of remaining competitive in an increasingly unfriendly environment.

True, all groups will benefit, whether they are different in terms of age, lifestyle, gender, or race. But their benefit is not the driving motivation. Managing diversity presumes that the driving force is the manager's, and the company's, self-interest.

Question: Where did the term "managing diversity" come from? Who originated the concept?

Answer: No one really knows who originated the concept. As I use the term, "managing" indicates the managerial approach—it's for and about *management*—and "diversity" simply reflects the reality of the work force today.

Question: Is managing diversity new or is it simply affirmative action warmed over?

Answer: Managing diversity is not warmed-over affirmative action. It is, instead, a different set of challenges and opportunities. It goes far beyond race and gender. And it is *new*—a process that hasn't yet been put on the agenda of America's companies. It's not that corporations have failed with managing diversity; they have not addressed it.

Question: Does managing diversity replace affirmative action? If not, how do they fit together?

Answer: Managing diversity will, in the long term, make affirmative action unnecessary. In the short term, corporations will need to do both in parallel. Managing diversity may make people more receptive to affirmative action, primarily because it suggests that there is an end to the tunnel.

Question: I've heard the term valuing differences, but I'm not sure exactly what it means or where it fits in.

Answer: Valuing differences initiatives are designed to enhance the individual's awareness, understanding, and acceptance of differences among people. In that it focuses on the individual and interpersonal levels, as opposed to the organizational level, it is similar to affirmative action. Typically, valuing differences does not involve the changing of corporate culture and systems as espoused by managing diversity.

Question: Why not simply skip affirmative action and valuing differences and go straight to managing diversity?

Answer: Managing diversity in a very real sense encompasses affirmative action and valuing differences, but there are two reasons why you can't ignore the more traditional modes.

The first is that implementing managing diversity to an extent where you can tap a substantial amount of its potential will take time. Just launching the managing diversity approach can take as long as five years. Full implementation and evaluation of results will take a minimum of ten years, more likely between fifteen and twenty years. So there must be ways to deal with diversity-related issues that arise while you are moving forward with managing diversity.

The second reason is that affirmative action and valuing differences have dealt with these issues in a way that has produced significant results. The difficulty is that they can't sustain them naturally. If you eliminate affirmative action and valuing differences before gaining the benefits of managing diversity, you risk having diversity-related issues not addressed. This will disadvantage people who are "different" and, more critically, it will affect the productivity of the organization.

Question: What is the likely scenario? Is it affirmative action, then valuing differences, then managing diversity—or can we go from affirmative action to managing diversity?

In other words, can you manage diversity without valuing differences?

Answer: You can manage diversity without valuing differences, but you can't manage diversity without understanding differences. The sequence that makes sense for me is that affirmative action must be followed by understanding and accepting differences, and then by managing diversity.

To say that managers must value differences before they can manage diversity implies that there is a choice, that managers who don't place a premium on diversity won't have to deal with it. But there is no choice. The reality is that whether you value diversity or not, you *will have it* as a major characteristic of your work force. If you are to be effective as a manager, you will have to manage diversity.

I also believe, however, that if you manage diversity effectively, you easily will come to value it.

Question: What kind of diversity does a manager see?

Answer: Although the most obvious sources of diversity are ethnicity, race, and gender, employees can differ along any number of lines. They may, for example, differ with respect to age, functional and educational backgrounds, lifestyle preferences, tenure within the organization, personality traits, and ways of thinking.

Obviously, they differ in numerous other ways as well. The significant differences for a given group of employees must be ferreted out empirically. They cannot be assumed or assigned, but must be identified through interactions with individual subordinates.

In determining how employees differ, managers must avoid stereotyping, positively or negatively. This may become more difficult as a manager gains experience with members of a given group and begins to believe that he "knows" what "they" are like.

Yet a manager always manages individuals, not groups. The most any manager can say is that "based on my experience *to date* with employees in my corporation, I have found certain characteristics to be shared; however, I understand that individuals differ, and that I cannot assume that these premises will hold true as I interact with additional members of a given racial, ethnic, or gender group. Instead, I must be open to the possibility that new members will be different."

Question: Why "managing" diversity rather than leveraging diversity or capitalizing diversity?

Answer: Because I begin from a managerial perspective. I define "managing" as the task of creating an environment that allows the individuals being managed to reach their full potential in pursuit of corporate objectives.

Through various legal, moral, and social responsibility mechanisms, we have created a diverse work force. Now we must ask ourselves whether we have the managerial know-how to tap the full potential of this entity that we have created.

Leveraging differences suggests that you're going to identify the differences people have and leverage those differences. This goes against the managing diversity concept. We're talking about managing a group of people who have both significant differences and significant similarities.

Question: Why managing diversity now? Why is this term coming up?

Answer: Diversity is becoming an issue not only because of the increasing percentage of minorities and women in the workplace but because of changing attitudes as well. In the past, people who were "different" were willing to assimilate, in order to get ahead in the workplace. Increasingly today, people are celebrating the things that make them different. They're more reluctant to put their differences on hold.

As a result, managers will find themselves dealing not with diversity but with unassimilated diversity. It is this *lack of assimilation* that creates the challenge. In the past, assimilation allowed us the luxury of having people who were different on the surface but homogeneous underneath. Now we must learn how to manage people who are different below the surface as well.

Question: Managing diversity doesn't say much about the richness of diversity and the benefits that can be gained from workplace diversity. Why is this? Aren't you ignoring a potentially strong motive for moving forward with managing diversity?

Answer: Many individuals believe that there is a richness in diversity that you can't get from a homogeneous work force. This may be true, but it's not necessary to support managing diversity. Whether there is a richness or not, managers *will* have employees with significant differences and similarities. The compelling case for managing diversity lies in the fact that diversity is a reality—or soon will be. By focusing on the richness, you risk suggesting that the manager has a choice. (The thinking goes, if you don't value this alleged richness, you don't have the need to move forward.)

Question: Are minorities and women naturally better at managing diversity?

Answer: No. It is easier to say that minorities and women may be more receptive to affirmative action and valuing differences because of the apparent benefits for them and also because of their experiences as minorities and women.

When it comes to diversity, however, most corporations have not asked anyone to manage in the real sense of the word. As a result, all managers are equally ill prepared. You might reasonably expect women and minorities to be sensitive to diversity issues, but being sensitive is not equivalent to managing.

Question: We have just spent years telling people that they should be color-blind. Now we're telling them to recognize and value the differences. Isn't this a major inconsistency?

Answer: No. The notions of color-blind and gender-blind never did call for ignoring the reality of differences. They simply insisted that we not discount or disadvantage a person because of his or her differences. In other words, neither color nor gender determined a person's worth.

Managing diversity calls for recognizing that people are different without condemning them for these differences. It also calls for taking these differences into account as managers determine what environment will allow diverse people to reach their full potential. Managing diversity is congruent with the true notions of color-blind and gender-blind.

Question: Women and minorities are just beginning to get something from affirmative action and now they are being asked to give that up for something that includes white males—who have always been advantaged. Isn't this unfair?

Answer: No. This question reflects the zero-sum nature of the traditional approach to diversity: that one group advances only at the expense of another. Remember, managing diversity isn't about doing something for employees. It's about enabling the manager for the benefit of the organization to tap the potential of *all* people. Including white males under the umbrella is not at the expense of anyone.

Question: What is going to prevent blacks from ending up on the bottom of the diversity pile?

Answer: Again, this reflects the zero-sum nature of the traditional approach. It also reflects a belief that somehow the system will work to the disadvantage of black employees.

Managing diversity is not based on a zero-sum assumption. A manager who practices managing diversity in a way that results in any group ending up on the bottom of the pile is not understanding the true sense of the concept.

Question: Won't managing diversity diffuse the effort now being devoted to race and gender issues?

Answer: This question normally is a reaction to the multiple dimensions of diversity. Often minorities and women will have difficulty seeing how a corporation that has not been able to handle two dimensions of diversity can now handle multiple dimensions. They fear that any progress in implementing the managing diversity concept will be at the expense of the attention traditionally given to race and gender issues. This is a real risk on a temporary, short-term basis. But as the manager gains expertise and capability in managing diversity, this risk will be mitigated.

It is also important to realize that true *sustainable* progress comes only when *all* of diversity's facets are addressed. Managing diversity is not a program. It calls for changing a way of life. Such a change cannot be selective; it happens across the board.

Question: We (white males) are being forced to change to accommodate them. They should change in order to fit in. We changed; why shouldn't they?

Answer: Willingness to be assimilated—to change in order to fit in—is an individual decision. For any number of reasons, different groups, whether they be white males with different lifestyles or ethnic or racial groups with different cultural back-grounds, are increasingly reluctant to accept assimilation.

So, as a manager, you have a choice. You can refuse to enter-tain the possibility that the corporation should adjust, and con-tinue to place the adaptation burden on the individual. But if you do that and individuals are unwilling to assimilate, their full po-tential will never be tapped. And if your competition is a com-pany that *is* willing to talk about a mutual adaptation process, you will soon find yourself at a disadvantage.

Question: I'm not clear about what you mean by assimila-tion. Can you give an example?

Answer: A manager of a department whose employees are predominantly Hispanics asked: "Is it too much to ask these peo-ple to speak English? We've given them the best job they've ever had." This is another way of asking, "Why won't these people assimilate and use our language?"

From a managing diversity perspective, where the manager's challenge and responsibility is to tap the full potential of all em-ployees, it's more valid to ask, "Is there a compelling business reason for these workers to speak English? Does the nature of their work require it? Is it too much to ask me to speak English and Spanish?" Managing diversity assumes that both the corpo-ration and its employees must adapt to each other.

All companies will and should require some individual ad-aptation. The challenge is to ensure that the prescriptions are es-sential to the integrity of the organization and not unnecessarily restrictive.

Question: From the perspective of senior management, how risky is empowerment management?

Answer: In the context of managing diversity, I make a ba-sic distinction between leadership and management. Leadership tasks include ensuring that the corporation is imbued with vision, that there is an articulated strategy (decisions designed to enable the corporation to gain a competitive advantage), and that there is an appropriate corporate culture. The outcomes of these three leadership tasks provide the context for carrying out managerial tasks.

The basic managerial task is to "bring in the bacon" in the short term—up to two years. There are at least two principal modes prescribing how a manager should do this: the doer and empowerment models. The empowerment model is practiced within the context of leadership. The more effectively the leadership tasks have been carried out, the more well-defined the context is for implementing the empowerment model.

In reality, if there is a clear vision and a very supportive and strong culture, empowerment management is much easier. In other words, leadership serves to socialize an individual employee with the essence of what the organization is about—the vision, the strategic rationale, and the basic critical assumptions that are driving the enterprise. When all this is understood by the individual, the risks of empowerment are greatly reduced. One of the main reasons managers are reluctant to empower is that they don't trust employees to function in a desirable way.

I believe that managers have a dual role: that of managing and that of leading. Leadership provides the context for management and in this way it also provides the context for empowerment.

Question: You put a lot of emphasis on changing cultural roots. What should be the roots of corporations that desire to move forward with managing diversity?

Answer: This is an empirical process question. In other words, managers must go through the process of examining their competitive environment and the nature of their business. They must then examine the present roots of their corporation in the context of these environmental realities.

Occasionally, personal preferences and strategic necessities conflict. One manager, confronted with the necessity for cultural change, said to me, "I like the roots of my company; they work for me." This is fine, but it misses the point. The issue is not whether the roots work for you and people like you, but rather whether they work for those who are not like you—whether they allow you as a manager to enable people who are different from yourself.

If the roots won't serve you well, you must determine what changes are needed in the existing culture. After that, you must develop a plan to direct the move from the present to the desired state. There is no substitute for this process. Implementing cultural change will require a commitment from managers to drive this change for at least a decade. Without the kind of individual commitment that develops as a result of going through the whole process, there can be no successful cultural change.

Question: What can I (senior management) do to change culture? What can I (middle management) do to change culture?

Answer: Senior managers often argue that their hands are tied because of middle managers. Middle managers say they can't do anything because of senior management. The reality is that both groups can contribute to the process of changing culture at their own level.

Managers at all levels must carry out both management and leading tasks. In practice, cultural change ultimately will require senior management's involvement and endorsement because of the magnitude of the effort. Yet it would be a serious mistake to assume that cultural change can be carried out solely at this level. The leadership tasks of building and maintaining a culture must occur throughout the pyramid. Each level of management must apply appropriate levers. These must be identified and action plans developed. In some instances they are basically the same levers but manifested differently.

Among the cultural change levers that *both* senior and middle managers must use are the following:

- Articulate the new roots at every opportunity.
- Ensure that systems are congruent with new roots.
- Create heroes/heroines who are supportive of new roots.
- Establish traditions (rites and rituals) supportive of new roots.
- Guard against managerial practices that are not supportive of the new roots.

These and other cultural change activities can't be confined to *any* level of management, but must prevail at *all* levels.

Question: Why isn't the "family" root appropriate in managing diversity? It has worked well for many corporations up to this point.

Answer: The notion that "we are family" is exclusive in nature—and that is the exact opposite of what managing diversity is about. The concepts of team and community are much more inclusive.

Also, the notion of family gives rise to a paternalistic climate where managers are like parents and employees are like children. This results in dependent behavior on the part of employees, and dependency is a major block to empowerment.

Even more important, the family model gives rise to the doer model: the manager [the parent] does the work and thereby shows the employees [the children] how the work should be done. This contrasts directly with the empowerment model. If you can't practice empowerment management, you can't practice managing diversity.

Question: How do you explain to middle-level managers the benefits of an empowerment style of management?

Answer: We must remember that all individuals aren't suited for management; some may be more suited as doers. This is not a negative statement; it's simply descriptive.

People are often made managers as a reward—they make a manager's higher salary but remain great doers. Corporations must devise ways of recognizing and compensating legitimate and effective doers without using management per se as a reward mechanism. They should then seek out individuals who have the skills and attitudes necessary to become empowerment managers.

Corporations that want to move to empowerment management must do much more than convince managers that they need to empower their people. They might need to do a major restructuring of the selection process for new managers, perhaps even redeploy some present ones.

Question: How do I get my managers to do the "right and proper" things?

Answer: This is fundamentally an educational process. (I don't mean training. Education deals with the way we think about issues; training deals with developing skills.) Progress must be made in changing the mindsets of individuals. If managers are to move forward with managing diversity, they will have to have mindset changes.

Question: My job is so demanding now that I don't have time as a manager to worry about this diversity stuff, and neither do my colleagues.

Answer: This is equivalent to saying, "I don't get paid to bring about cultural change; I get paid to deliver results." Managers who make this statement are indicating that they have described their job in the "doer" model mode. And in reality, doer managers *don't* have time. The only way to get around the time constraints is to change the concept and priorities of the manager's job. It takes a manager who accepts the reality of *leadership* tasks to agree to spend the time and energy needed to implement cultural change.

Question: What do you do when management seems to have no motivation at all to move forward in managing diversity?

Answer: Managing diversity is not for everyone. It requires either vision or the presence of pain. Corporations that have a vision of the future and an understanding of the implications of the changing work-force demographics and attitudes can understand the opportunities presented by managing diversity. Similarly, corporations experiencing pain with diversity at this time can appreciate the necessity. Without vision or pain, however, there is not likely to be sufficient motivation to pioneer with a concept such as managing diversity.

Even when there is vision or pain, a corporation's managers may be reluctant to pioneer because pioneering is incongruent with their corporate culture or individual natures. These managers must wait until others have established a track record with managing diversity before they jump on board. This means, however, that they probably won't be able to tap managing diversity as a strategic opportunity because many corporations will be far ahead of them. They will jump on the bandwagon simply to keep up with the competition rather than staying ahead.

Question: Can anything be done without senior management's commitment?

Answer: Yes. The press for managing diversity can begin anywhere and, in practice, often does. Ultimately, given the nature and magnitude of the change we're discussing, senior management's commitment will be necessary, especially in a doer, paternalistic organization. But the beginning of exploring managing diversity and of recognizing its potential benefits can occur at any place in the organization. What's important is that individual managers who press for the implementation of managing diversity recognize that they must eventually impress and influence senior management to become committed.

Question: Little has been said about subordinates and managing diversity. What role do they play?

Answer: Subordinates can play a major role in furthering the implementation of managing diversity. Central to this role is accepting, understanding, and appreciating differences among employees, since they will be part of a work force characterized by unassimilated diversity.

Subordinates must also help managers identify, appreciate, and understand differences among employees. They must be willing to foster quality communication lines between managers and themselves. Finally, subordinates must accept some responsibility for implementing managing diversity. They must agree to share the change agent role. Without informed, committed subordinates, managers cannot launch or sustain major, long-term change.

Question: What about support groups? Are they compatible with managing diversity?

Answer: Support groups have been very effective in many corporations. However, once managing diversity has been fully implemented, you wouldn't expect to see them. These groups evolve when people feel the need to interact with people who are similar. When people feel that the overall environment supports their efforts, they are less likely to need additional supports. In this context, support groups are transitional mechanisms as corporations move from traditional programs to a managing diversity approach.

Question: How does meritocracy—the presumption that "cream will rise to the top"—fit with the concept of managing diversity? Are they in conflict?
Answer: No. Our research suggests that merit promotions have three dimensions:

1. Task merit: Demonstrated capability to perform a given task sufficiently.
2. Cultural merit: Demonstrated capability to conform to the major requirements of the corporation's basic assumptions or roots.
3. Political merit: Demonstrated capability to attract the endorsement of someone with sufficient clout to minimize doubt about an individual's qualifications.

People who are "different" often are able to meet the first condition but not the second or third.

Managing diversity simply calls for the manager to ensure that cultural and political realities do not advantage or disadvantage anyone because of irrelevant considerations. In this sense, then, there is no conflict between the two ideas.

Notice that this merit framework makes it clear that cream does not rise naturally. All employees, even "self-made" individuals, benefit from political assists. This is the nature of organizational reality. This explains why "just do your job; don't get involved in politics" is bad advice. New managers who follow this advice often wonder why they are overlooked for promotions. There is no substitute for fulfilling all three requirements of the merit framework.

Question: Can you point to any success stories with managing diversity?
Answer: Managing diversity is an embryonic, pioneering concept. Some corporations have been successful in launching

managing diversity efforts, but I cannot point to any corporation where managing diversity is a "done deal." It is simply too early.

Indeed, if I could identify corporations where managing diversity is a reality, it would invalidate one of the most significant points: *managing diversity can be the source of strategic opportunity.* The more success stories there are, the less the strategic opportunity becomes. Inherent in the notion of strategic is the assumption of doing something others haven't been able to do.

Question: How do you measure managing diversity's success?

    Answer: You begin by asking the appropriate questions. *Don't* ask, "How many minorities and women do we have at each level of the organization?" or "How good is our representation of minorities and women in the corporation?" These are important questions, but they're not the best questions for determining whether you're making progress in managing diversity.

You must be clear that the goal of managing diversity is to tap the full potential of *all* employees. You want to measure your progress by getting a sense of how well you are tapping this potential, or at least developing an environment that ultimately will allow you to do so. A major premise of managing diversity, for example, is that you must have an appropriate culture and systems. So, to measure the progress of managing diversity, you must determine the extent to which your systems are supportive of a diverse work force.

We need ways to measure both the appropriateness of the culture with respect to a diverse work force and the effectiveness of a set of systems in serving such a work force. Here are some of the questions we should be asking:

- To the extent that women and minorities are advancing in the corporation, is it happening naturally or are special facilitative efforts required? (As a company develops and refines its managing diversity capabilities, its reliance on special initiatives for minorities and women will drop.)
- To what degree have managers reduced their reliance on assimilation as the principal option for approaching diver-

sity? What indications are there that mutual adjustment of
the individual and the corporation is viewed as legitimate?

- To what extent are managers using a combination of the
doer and empowerment models, as opposed to relying primarily on the doer model? (If you're not sure about this,
the following two questions often indicate the degree to
which managers are doers.) Are mangers evaluated and rewarded on the basis of their ability to develop people? To
what do your managers really put their attention?

- To what extent have cultural roots been modified in the direction that will facilitate progress with managing diversity? Specifically, what actions have been taken to implement the root changes? Are the changes clear to
employees? Are employees beginning to accept the
changes and their implications?

We have not yet reached the stage of implementing evaluation technologies. But when they evolve, they must be grounded
in the understanding that it is necessary to assess whether the
corporate culture and systems are becoming multicultural rather
than remaining monocultural. Multicultural reflects the reality of
diversity; monocultural reflects the preferences and nature of the
dominant group.

Notes

Chapter 1

1. William B. Johnston and Arnold H. Packer. *Workforce 2000: Work and Workers for the 21st Century*. Indianapolis: Hudson Institute, 1987.
2. Paul Richter. "Clash Over Culture at Time Inc. Hearing." The *Los Angeles Times*, July 12, 1989, section IV, page 1.
3. Edgar H. Schein. *Organizational Culture and Leadership*. San Francisco: Jossey-Bass, 1985, pages 1–22.

Chapter 8

1. Rafael Aguayo. *Dr. Deming: The American Who Taught the Japanese About Quality*. New York: Carol Publishing Group, 1990.
2. For a discussion of the various approaches to total quality, see Roland A. Dumas, Nancy Cushing, and Carol Laughlin. "Making Quality Control Theories Workable." *Training and Development Journal*, 24 (February 1987), pages 30–33.
3. Andrea Gabor. *The Man Who Discovered Quality*. New York: Times Books, 1990, page 29.
4. Comments made during interview with author.
5. Beverly Geber. "Quality Circles: The Second Generation." *Training*, 23 (December 1986), pages 56–57.
6. A Corning publication entitled "Corning Total Quality Digest" reports on the company's efforts and progress.
7. Remarks made in a video presentation describing some of Avon's training efforts around managing diversity.
8. W. Edwards Deming. *Out of the Crisis*. Cambridge, Massachusetts: Massachusetts Institute of Technology, 1986, pages 153–154.

Index